STRIPER HOT SPOTS

NEW ENGLAND

STRIPER HOT SPOTS

NEW ENGLAND

FRANK DAIGNAULT

BURFORD BOOKS

Printed in the United States of America.

10   9   8   7   6   5   4   3   2   1

Library of Congress Cataloging-in-Publication data is on file with the Library of Congress.

Manufactured in the United States of America

CONTENTS

Block Island

Martha's Vineyard

Nantucket

Cape Cod Canal

Mainland Massachusetts

How the Spots Rate for Fishing
(5 is the highest)

	Rating	Inlet	Jetty	Fly Fishing	ORV Advisable
1. Calf Pasture Point	2			X	
2. Cedar Point Compo Beach	3			X	
3. Penfield Reef	3	X		X	
4. Saint Mary's Ash Creek	2				
5. Housatonic River	1	X	X	X	
6. Silver Sands S.P.	3	X		X	
7. Enfield Dam	3				
8. Hammonasset Beach S.P.	2	X	X		
9. Cornfield Point	3	X		X	
10. Conn. DEP Headquarters	2	X	X	X	
11. Sound View Beach	3	X	X	X	
12. Niantic River	3	X	X	X	
13. Harkness Memorial	3	X		X	
14. Thames River, Norwich	2				
15. Bluff Point S.P.	1				
16. Napatree Point	2	X	X	X	
17. Watch Hill	1	X			
18. Weekapaug Breachway	2	X	X	X	
19. "Quonnie" Breachway	4	X	X	X	X
20. East Beach, Charlestown	2	X			
21. Charlestown Breachway	4	X	X	X	
22. Green Hill	1	X			
23. Deep Hole	3	X		X	
24. Harbor of Refuge	4	X	X	X	
25. Point Judith	2	X	X		
26. Narragansett	3				
27. Narrow River	3	X	X	X	
28. Beavertail	2				
29. Rome Point	2	X	X	X	

		Rating	Inlet	Jetty	Fly Fishing	ORV Advisable
30.	Providence River	🐟🐟	✗			
31.	Barrington River	🐟🐟	✗	✗	✗	
32.	Warren River	🐟🐟	✗	✗	✗	
33.	Colt Drive	🐟	✗	✗	✗	
34.	Bristol Narrows	🐟🐟	✗	✗	✗	
35.	Brenton Point	🐟				
36.	Fort Adams	🐟				
37.	Southwest Point, B.I.	🐟🐟🐟				
38.	Mohegan Bluffs, B.I.	🐟🐟🐟				
39.	Southeast Light, B.I.	🐟				
40.	Grove Point, B.I.	🐟🐟				
41.	Inlet to Great Salt Pond, B.I.	🐟🐟🐟🐟	✗	✗	✗	
42.	Vineyard Bridges, M.V.	🐟🐟🐟	✗	✗	✗	
43.	Wasque Point, M.V.	🐟🐟🐟🐟🐟	✗			
44.	Squibnocket Point. M.V.	🐟🐟🐟🐟🐟				
45.	Gay Head Cliffs, M.V.	🐟🐟🐟				
46.	Lobsterville Beach, M.V.	🐟🐟🐟🐟	✗	✗	✗	
47.	Brant Point, Nantucket	🐟🐟🐟🐟	✗	✗	✗	
48.	Eel Point, Nantucket	🐟🐟🐟🐟	✗	✗	✗	✗
49.	Smith Point, Nantucket	🐟🐟🐟🐟	✗	✗	✗	✗
50.	Surfside Beach, Nantucket	🐟🐟	✗			✗
51.	Great Point, Nantucket	🐟🐟🐟	✗			✗
52.	Herring Run, Cape Cod Canal	🐟	✗	✗		
53.	Mass. Maritime, C.C. Canal	🐟🐟	✗	✗	✗	
54.	Mud Flats, C.C. Canal	🐟🐟	✗	✗	✗	
55.	East End (Scusset), C.C. Canal	🐟🐟🐟	✗	✗	✗	
56.	Westport River	🐟🐟🐟	✗	✗	✗	
57.	South Cape Beach	🐟🐟	✗	✗	✗	
58.	Nauset Beach	🐟🐟🐟🐟	✗	✗		✗
59.	Chatham Inlet—North Edge	🐟🐟🐟	✗	✗	✗	✗
60.	Chatham Inlet—South Side	🐟🐟🐟🐟	✗	✗	✗	
61.	Nauset Inlet	🐟🐟🐟🐟	✗	✗	✗	

	Rating	Inlet	Jetty	Fly Fishing	ORV Advisable
62. Outer Cape	🐟🐟🐟🐟				
63. Provincelands	🐟🐟🐟	✗	✗	✗	✗
64. Race Point	🐟🐟🐟🐟🐟	✗	✗	✗	✗
65. Pamet River	🐟🐟🐟	✗	✗	✗	
66. Sandy Neck	🐟🐟	✗	✗	✗	✗
67. Hull Gut	🐟🐟	✗			
68. Boston Harbor Islands	🐟🐟🐟	✗		✗	
69. Deer Island	🐟🐟	✗		✗	
70. Boston North Shore	🐟🐟🐟	✗		✗	
71. Plum Island	🐟🐟🐟🐟🐟	✗	✗	✗	
72. Hampton River Inlet	🐟🐟	✗	✗	✗	
73. General Sullivan Bridge	🐟🐟🐟🐟	✗			
74. Mousam River	🐟🐟🐟	✗	✗	✗	
75. Saco River	🐟🐟🐟	✗	✗	✗	
76. Old Orchard Beach	🐟				
77. Scarborough River Marsh	🐟🐟🐟	✗	✗	✗	
78. Spurwink River	🐟🐟🐟🐟	✗	✗	✗	
79. Martin Point Bridge	🐟🐟	✗			
80. Popham Beach	🐟🐟🐟🐟	✗	✗	✗	
81. Morse River	🐟🐟🐟🐟	✗	✗	✗	
82. Kennebec River	🐟🐟	✗	✗	✗	
83. Penobscot River	🐟	✗	✗	✗	

ACKNOWLEDGMENTS

While I claim full credit for the formulation of this book's concept, purpose, and execution, there are any number of contributors without whose able assistance *Striper Hot Spots* would never have come to be. Early in the project, I sought the help of some trusted friends on the Striper Coast. In exchange for their familiarity with certain sections of the shore, I promised each of them a coffee-table copy of the finished work and a guaranteed mention of their contribution within its pages to show their grandchildren; in addition, they have the knowledge that they contributed something to a sport I was already certain they loved. South to north, please applaud the following:

Captain Ray DeCosta for his lifetime of experience on Nantucket, and I owe a debt to Bill Pew for many of the details there that I never thought to ask DeCosta about. If there was a Nantucket book, they could have coauthored it. Kay Moulton of Surfland Newburyport rattled off the whole story on Plum Island; what a racket I could have had with eighty-two more like her. The late Dr. Robert Post, author of that fine treatise on the Vineyard's legendary surf fishers, *Reading the Water,* didn't just tell me about fishing there, he wrote about it. Another professional writer, and faithful longtime friend, Matt Zajac, penned much of the material on Connecticut. Then, Ron Rozsa, a biologist for Long Island Sound Programs, and Rod Macleod, a biologist for Connecticut Marine Fisheries, wrapped that state up, all three assuring me that their participation was a privilege. Dick Pinney of the *Manchester Union Leader,* looking at the back of his hand to conjure up New Hampshire's hot spots, rattled them off like the names of his children.

Lastly, Billy Gardner of Portland gave me half of Maine and corrected any errors that I might have made from my own research there. Even my daughter, Susan Daignault, who is now a Mainer, led me to Fort Popham long before this book's conception. All these people have been the cat's meow.

It will surprise no one from the beaches and gun clubs of New England who knows me that my wife, Joyce, rules upon everything written here from the initial concept to its final execution. Imagine having a high school sweetheart who becomes your wife, lover, companion in the woods and on the beaches, and mothers four beautiful children for you along the way. Then, just when you think it can't get any better, she assists in the production of your books. What a joy she has been for our fifty-three years together. Scary that I need her so much.

Here's one of seven 50-pound-plus stripers that I have taken in my 50 years of surfcasting. (1969 photo)

INTRODUCTION

The purpose of this book is to document the finest surfcasting locations of the New England Striper Coast from the Hudson River to Central Maine. It is a directory of prime places to go fishing. It contains directions, geographic considerations, fishing methods in use, favored angling times and someone to call upon for advice. There are, of course, any number of shore-fishing locations outside these parameters, but I have chosen these because social and natural considerations render them the most reasonable.

The main criteria for the selection of these hot spots are their productivity and accessibility. I define productivity here as a surfcaster's potential for success as compared with other locations. Success, of course, can be based upon the catching of any number of gamefish, and these can be ranked according to species most often sought, those most important. The guiding considerations here, which should surprise no seasoned saltwater angler, are, in rank order: striped bass, bluefish, weakfish, blackfish, fluke, cod, bonito, and porgy. While this leaves out some species, I think the spirit of my intent has been served. Of course, if stripers were the only game in town, this book would be limited to them alone. Indeed, with some exceptions, if it isn't a striper spot, it doesn't count. But so often, a place that appeals to one fish appeals to another, as is the case when adding bluefish and weakfish. Similarly, some locations where the striper is locally important have a unique run of another species and the secondary gamefish is often overlooked; still another is famous for blackfish but overlooked for its fine striper fishing. I have tried to cover all that is known.

What this book is not is a treatise on surfcasting. You are expected to have learned that elsewhere, or to be engaged in the lifelong pursuit of this knowledge. You are supposed to know how to deal with slick jetties and sloppy salt-chuck—often green, white, and dirty—blowing over the jetty, which is the only thing between you and your maker. Korkers, cleats, belts, flotation, and judgment are outside the bounds of this book. It is assumed that you know that surfcasting can be quite dangerous.

It is not enough to list all these places without extensive supportive information. Techniques and conditions play no small part in the formulation of a hot spot, as well as what is needed to make it all work. The selection of technique becomes a case of choosing between what one thinks is best versus what is being done locally. I tend to go with the latter, on the assumption that the anglers

who frequent a spot know more than I about what works there. No seasoned regular would argue that most places enjoy sets of favored conditions that often improve or ruin the fishing. For instance, a sou'west wind at Race Point during a given stage of tide might enhance one's opportunities; conversely, an east wind might ruin all hope on a particular east-facing beach—though not on all east-facing beaches. To make matters more complicated, there might even be an interrelationship between methods and conditions: for example, if everybody says that pink Nackajimas work best at a given place during a southeast wind, that is the way it gets written up.

Another consideration for inclusion here is that it has never been our intent to document some little hot spot that accommodates two esoteric hardcores doing a striper number alone in the dark of night.

Not because secrecy is important or that I take anyone's threats seriously, but such disclosures would serve no purpose. As a result, public property predominates (70 percent of hot spots) because of its inherent accessibility. Conversely, some places are more popular than they deserve to be simply because they accommodate greater numbers of fishermen.

When I take into account all the factors—size, accessibility, species availability, water movement and depth, facing directions, and overall production in terms of fish caught—each hot spot begs for some sort of value judgment that defines it more objectively. Indeed, to keep the information that gathers on a particular spot in control, a rating system serves as a means of boiling it all down. Here, I must quickly create a clear separation between a 5-mile hot spot at the mouth of a river, like Plum Island, and some obscure beach a mile long that is rarely fished—and all the levels in between. What springs from those thoughts is that Race Point is rated a five while "Little Beach" is a one. Of course, such judgments can become mighty subjective while inspiring heated disagreements—as often based on local pride as on protectionist sentiments. With those thoughts in mind, I am tempted to apologize in advance for decisions that might seem skewed to some knowing regular out there. My rating system breaks down as follows:

Rating	Number of Hot Spots with That Rating
5	4
4	17
3	25
2	26
1	11

If I dare believe that this book will enjoy any life after its initial release, I must take into account the influence of time upon species.

All gamefish are inexorably destined to rise and fall in availability as years go by. Certainly, striped bass—at this writing—are at heretofore unknown levels of high population, due to some lucky reproductive seasons, better management, and restoration efforts. Bluefish, I have learned through extensive examination of historical accounts, seem to be subject to fifty-year cycles. In the 1960s, many surfcasters could not identify one, but by the 1970s, blues were seen in Maine for the first time in one hundred years. It is known that a species extends its range only when at a peak in its population, and while there is no need to elaborate further about today's bluefish angling opportunities, I must emphasize that those opportunities have never remained historically constant, nor will they.

In my lifetime, I have seen the rise and subsequent fall of gray weakfish (*Cynoscion regalis*) twice. The reasons cited for this variation include natural cycles and overfishing. They are now at a relative low in their cycle and are rare in the northern part of their range but increasing in New Jersey. By contrast, variations in the blackfish population seem far less dramatic. While the above examples make the point, I will date myself here by saying that fluke, or summer flounder, are in decline . . . again; black sea bass are coming back; scup are as thick as insects; and cod and pollack are so overfished commercially that they are rare at the beach, whereas at one time I used to catch them all winter in the surf. My point here is that just because a species is listed at a spot does not mean that it will be available the year you happen to fish there. I am, however, tempted to say that there will always be something, because it appears that the demise of one species seems always to be a signal for the advance of another. Even the bait species, so central to each creature's existence, experience rises and declines in population; this implies some larger cyclical pattern for everything living in the ocean, but adequate explanation is still elusive. I hasten to underscore that baitfish cycles have a direct bearing on the behavior of those species we seek.

This book contains four distinct kinds of information: (1) observations that are entirely my own and for which I bear sole responsibility, as with the stretch from Watch Hill to Race Point; (2) information that is a combination of personal experience and research, in which I depended upon some input from others, such as with Maine; (3) sections that are completely the result of research, for which I began by interviewing qualified respondents and then checked the information for accuracy, as with Connecticut, and Nantucket; and (4) sections that were written by others and then reviewed by me, as is the case with Martha's Vineyard and some parts of Connecticut. As one might guess, the greatest danger lies with outside input, which was occasionally colored by evasive tactics to protect a spot.

One of my fears is that some of this fact distortion could have slipped through. Not so much that a spot might have been skipped because apparently cooperative advisers were steering an agenda, but, rather, because surfcasters were out to protect their home turf. Indeed, out-and-out refusal to cooperate would have been more welcome, and I had some of that.

Block Island got more protection than it deserved. That was in keeping with the overt behavior by its protectors that has characterized it since its discovery as a viable, though often overstated, striper hot spot. Smashed windshields and slashed tires in the past have too many people running scared, while others suggest that bypassing the Block entirely would be safer. Of course, its obvious omission would have been tantamount to encasing it in neon and would have brought it to the attention of every surfcaster this side of Australia. There was so much stonewalling that my first investigation was rendered worthless. After a second examination of Block Island, I still don't trust the information, partly because no one was willing to risk mention of his or her name in the acknowledgments section here. What few remember and most never knew is that the first article I ever published, "Block Island Safari" (*Salt Water Sportsman*, August 1970), expounded upon the great bluefishing from shore there at a time when the species was still quite scarce, as well as the suspicion that bass fishing was not exactly shabby when productive striper fishing was discovered in Mohegan Bluffs in July of '69 by our son and me. So much for secrecy.

The notion of "spot burning" is applied by some anglers to the act of publicizing a fishing location. The logic employed is that the less known about where fishing is going on, the less competition is likely to ensue over fishing there. What many seem to want is obscure and overlooked fishing hot spots that are devoid of other anglers so that those multitudes may enjoy them themselves. But such utopias are not really attainable in a densely populated geographic setting as can be found in what is now known as our Striper Coast. Indeed, the true secrets of the shorelines frequented by knowing disciples of the striper surf are not where to fish but rather, how to fish them. As long as we deal with mapped shorelines, global positioning, mass media, Internet communication and a plethora of printed media devoted to striper fishing, I fail to see any true secrets, especially when so many of the well-documented locations are public property promulgated for recreation. All that is being done here is your legwork.

The late Frank Woolner, who was my first editor and mentor 40 years ago, wrote a sensitive and telling piece about this very subject back when Sophia Loren was first learning about men. In his "To Kill a Lake" Woolner lamented the agonies of publicizing a great and somewhat private fishing spot. His point was that those of us who write about exciting opportunities in the field are apt to draw the multitudes and destroy the very thing we love most. You can only do so much of the gimmickry of old-time war correspondents "somewhere in Southeast Asia" or the angling scribe's "a small stream in Allegheny County." Thus, discussions that pinpoint what is good become matters of conscience for outdoor writers struggling with objectivity, secrecy and what others are likely to say in their expository prose. Location, as the real estate agents like to say, is everything. And the old saw about information really being the farmer's daughter hits you right between the eyes. If you don't do it someone else will.

Striper Hot Spots is nothing more than some badly needed musical chairs that engages the same number of seats while changing the rumps. This broadening of people's available locations will have no adverse influence upon the quality of the sport.

Nearly all to whom I spoke were truthful, said so when they didn't know, and told me where I could find out. They were usually thrilled to participate in this endeavor, which should certainly outlast me and probably some of them. Smart enough to know, without being reminded, that they were contributing something, they were enthusiastic, truthful, and flattered to have the opportunity.

Examining some of the common qualities of the 83 locations yielded some not-so-surprising statistics. For instance, 60 percent of them are inlets. I have long said, always practiced, and on many occasions written on the beauty of inlets as places where bait lured great gamefish. Because so many inlets are flanked by jetties to preserve their integrity, 20 percent of the spots ended up being flanked by jetties. That 63 percent of the spots host fly fishing speaks more of the trendy nature of the activity. Truth is that one could fly fish them all, but I tried to stay with either personal experience or that of respondents. The use of over-sand vehicles is permitted in 18 percent of the places, but that is not to say that a "beach buggy" is needed to fish there in all cases. They are truly necessary for only ten spots on the Cape and islands.

There is an evolution going on in the acceptance of a place being known as a hot spot that is natural in some cases. Chatham Inlet, now split, refines the best in this directory; and the Boston North Shore is being added to because of harbor pollution abatements. A dozen other spots have been rewritten extensively with more pertinent information. In response to the overwhelming interest in fly fishing, we have made a greater effort to identify the growing list of suitable fly-fishing locations. Fly fishers should watch for the special fly icon, which designates hot spots known for fly fishing. Each of the hot spots has a contact tip—a fishing shop you can call. Thankfully some of them serve more than one location, which means there are more places to fish than shops to advise us.

The hot spots are listed in geographical order, from south to north, as the migrating species travel. So if you don't like to read a book in order, or if you just plain like to jump around, feel free to do that here.

CONNECTICUT

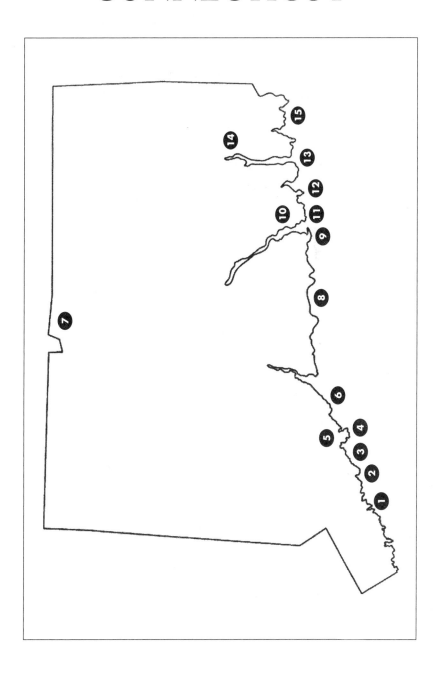

Connecticut

Private ownership of the shoreline reduces Connecticut's attractiveness as a shore fishing location. Indeed, nearly all the spots listed here are within the bounds of state parks. No doubt there is excellent fishing in any number of other places, but local private control prevents access through a complicated variety of ordinances, selectively enforced parking regulations, and illegally hidden rights-of-way. Thus, and this is by no means unique to Connecticut, access opportunities are better for nearby residents, who enjoy circumvention and immunity. Usually, when our sweethearts wish us luck, they're referring to the fishing; for Connecticut they mean the parking.

Having said this, I am, nevertheless, pleased to report that the public property that emerges from my research is well chosen. A more dispassionate critic would probably regard the spots I've listed for Connecticut as exemplars of "multiple use," but I can't shake the feeling that they were either chosen by a fisherman or chosen with fishing uppermost in mind. Good fishing is no small criterion for the siting of state parks in this state. Modern policies, which will influence access in the future, favor a more reasonable balance in utilization of coastal resources. Today, waterfront sites have to provide meaningful public access, and the shore-bound angler can look forward to greater access opportunities as a result.

Unique to this chapter is the fact that government input was greater here than in any other state. First, Ron Rozsa, a biologist for Long Island Sound Programs and an enthusiastic shore fisherman as well as striperman, read some of the copy during its preparation and directed me to an even better source in Rod Macleod, a biologist for Connecticut Marine Fisheries. With Macleod's input I had so many hot spots that the cuts list was nearly as long as the list of places

I've described—not because Connecticut is superior, but because my information for this state was so complete and derived in such measure from professional sources. It's what these guys do.

Another anomaly that I bumped into, much to my delight, is that this state is awash with saltwater fly fishers. Thus, while it is not the case, the notion that Connecticut's fly fishing is better than elsewhere emerges here, more as a result of local insistence than natural conditions.

What fun fishing you could have going to the places that have failed to make the cut. I commend the following to your indulgence with the reminder that all the judgments in this book are ultimately subjective:

Greenwich Point Park, Stamford
Shippan Point, Stamford
Sherwood Island State Park, Westport
Pleasure Beach/Town Pier, Bridgeport
Long Beach, Stratford/Bridgeport
Stratford Point, Stratford
Power Plant on the Housatonic, Devon
Milford Harbor East and West Jetties
Sandy Point, West Haven
Noank Town Dock
Rocky Neck State Park, Old Lyme
Black Hall River Bridge

1

Calf Pasture Point and Town Pier
South Norwalk, Connecticut

BEST MONTHS TO FISH: March through June, and September through November.

RECOMMENDED METHODS: Chunks, plugs, fly fishing, and sea worms.

FISH YOU CAN EXPECT TO CATCH: Stripers, bluefish, and some blackfish.

HOW TO GET THERE: Take exit 16 off I–95 and turn left at the traffic light onto East Avenue. Follow East Avenue to a traffic circle, then bear right onto Gregory Boulevard. Take a right onto Ludlow Parkway and follow it to its end.

People who fish the town pier like to use cut bait (chunks) of menhaden, herring, or mackerel held on the bottom with a sinker. The popularity of this spot would preclude any opportunity for lure fishing during all but the deepest hours of the night. Best tide phase at this spot is high water, when it is not possible to fish the bar out front. The pier is also popular in September for snapper blues when they are at a point in their development of inch-per-week growth. Look for some decent winter flounder fishing in March with sea worms. There is some blackfish fishing, but that is not what has made this spot.

On the bar out front, the gang enjoys plugging swimmers like Rebels, Mambo Minnows, and Red Fins tied direct. Wading is not possible until the tide is down to around halfway. If the fishing proves to be any good, regulars will stay until rising water forces them off; the drop, because of combining currents of the Norwalk River, has an edge. Protected by the Norwalk Islands, the bar is popular with fly fishermen. As with the pier, if there is room and water is low enough for a sand spike, some people will chunk from the bar.

John Baldino, fishing from a boat in the Norwalk Islands right off Calf Pasture Point, landed a 71-pound striper only a few years ago. This proves that the big mamas can be there.

During daylight, a town parking permit is required between Memorial Day and Labor Day, but fishing is open to anyone after closing time. There are fewer hassles in spring and fall.

CONTACT TIP: Call Fisherman's World, (203) 866-1075, for Calf Pasture Point information.

2
Cedar Point and Compo Beach
Westport, Connecticut

BEST MONTHS TO FISH: March through June, and September through November.

RECOMMENDED METHODS: Swimming plugs, cut baits, sea worms, and fly fishing.

FISH YOU CAN EXPECT TO CATCH: Stripers and bluefish.

HOW TO GET THERE: From exit 18 off I–95, get onto the Sherwood Island State Park Connector northbound, then take a left (west) onto Green Farms Road. A left onto Hills Point Road leads to the beach. Take a right (south) onto Compo Road, then take the next left for the entrance.

These two spots are combined because they are adjacent and fished and spoken of by locals in the same breath. Cedar Point is a little more protected at the river mouth, while Compo Beach is more open to the Sound. Opportunities here reflect those at Calf Point. Differences often develop around the type and location of baitfish that have drawn gamefish here in the first place. It is a case of who has the bait where the bunkers happen to be. Naturally, the influence of the Saugatuck River at the west end (Cedar Point) holds an edge for the dropping tide, but the open water and stony shore of Slates, on the east end of Compo, more than compensate for that.

Depending on the winds, the fly fishers prefer the river mouth, and so much the better if the tide is dropping. There is enough space here for you to fish bait or plug, with some anglers doing both—plugging with their eye on a baited rod. At the west end of Compo Beach, in front of the cannons, there is a serious blackfish run spring and fall. Tackle shops say to block out early May and late October on your calendar.

As at Calf Pasture, summer hassles and parking stickers are the rule, but the best fishing is at the two quiet ends of the season. While there may not be any 70-pounders on the record books for this hot spot, all agree it rates one better than Calf Pasture.

CONTACT TIP: Call the Sportsman's Den, (203) 869-3234, for more on Cedar Point and Calf Pasture.

3
Penfield Reef
Fairfield, Connecticut

BEST MONTHS TO FISH: May through November.
RECOMMENDED METHODS: Fly fishing and swimming plugs.

FISH YOU CAN EXPECT TO CATCH: Stripers and bluefish.

HOW TO GET THERE: Take exit 22 from I–95 to Round Hill Road to Route 1; then take a right. At the traffic light, take a left onto Reef Road, which leads to the Sound. Parking is available at a recreation park on the left side. Across the road, on the left, about 50 yards past the stop sign, there is a walkway between two houses, which, after ¼ mile, leads to a beach walkway.

Connecticut shores are loaded with top-notch night spots.

Penfield Reef is a rock-and-cobble sand spit that extends into Long Island Sound for about a mile. During low tide, the spit is exposed enough for fishermen in waders to follow it down. Thus, this place is popular during a falling tide. One of the few spots where fly fishing leads the way, it remains a good place for plug fishermen who utilize swimming plugs during the night.

Of course, the above rules are not hard and fast. Cut baits can be used— tackle shops say that live eels are becoming increasingly popular, and no doubt there are other species available at selected locations. Those who know their way around here in the dark of night do use the flood tide to their advantage, but until you know the ropes, I would not advise you to chance getting confused in a rising tide and getting trapped in deep water.

CONTACT TIP: Call the Sportsman's Den, (203) 869-3234, for angling inquiries.

4

Saint Mary's Beach, Ash Creek, and Henry J. Moore Fishing Pier
Fairfield, Connecticut

BEST MONTHS TO FISH: April through November.

RECOMMENDED METHODS: Cut bait (menhaden, herring, or mackerel) and swimming plugs.

FISH YOU CAN EXPECT TO CATCH: Stripers, bluefish, blackfish, and fluke.

HOW TO GET THERE: Ash Creek and the Moore Fishing Pier are at the South Benson Marina. From I–95 take exit 23 to Route 1 south. Take a left (after McDonald's) onto South Benson Road, then a left onto Oil Field Road, then a right onto Turney Road to the marina. For Saint Mary's Beach, take exit 25 off I–95 onto Fairfield Avenue south. Take a left at Gillman Street and continue to the east side of Ash Creek. Parking and access are provided.

Saint Mary's Beach faces the open Long Island Sound where the bottom is composed of boulders and rocks. Across from the beach is the Henry J. Moore Fishing Pier, which is actually an extension of a rip-rap embankment bordering Ash Creek Channel. The channel is popular with stripermen who watch the creek at night for feeding linesides that gorge on bait there, particularly during a falling tide. Menhaden schools frequent Ash Creek and are often trapped in the marina basin by predators. Blues exhibit the same behavior as stripers but are more likely than stripers to do so in daylight. For day anglers, there is a good fluke run in the channel out front during the late summer and early fall. The rocky bottom of Saint Mary's appeals to blackfish in spring, when their spawning run is on. Look for them the third week in April and use sea worms. Many wanted to rate this spot a three for stripers—a tough call.

CONTACT TIP: St. Mary's Beach, Ash Creek information is available at Ted's (203) 366-7615.

5

Housatonic River
Stratford, Connecticut

BEST MONTHS TO FISH: April, May, October, November.
RECOMMENDED METHODS: Plugs and fly fishing.
FISH YOU CAN EXPECT TO CATCH: Stripers and blues, plus a mixed bag upriver.
HOW TO GET THERE: From Route 95, take exit 34 south for ¹⁄₁₀ mile, turn right onto Bridgeport Avenue, then go ½ mile left on Naugatuck Avenue. Drive ½ mile to a right on Milford Point Road. It is a mile to Laurel Beach, and from there you can follow the shore southwest until you reach the Audubon gate.

The Housatonic River is another of those environmental success stories underlined by both cleaner water and effective fisheries management. The spot's coverage here is really a river system, which zeros in on two locations: the mouth of the "Housey" at Milford Point in Stratford on the river's east bank; and the first upstream dam in Darby, which marks the end of tidewater and stops fish from any further upstream migration. The Milford Point location is the most important as it relates to saltwater striper fishing.

Here, at the mouth of the river, strong tidal currents sweep past Milford Point. On the dropping tide the 750-acre tidal marsh of Nells Island, with its numerous salt creeks, keeps a steady dole of estuarine baitfish sweeping past the point. The island itself is state property operated as the Charles E. Wheeler Wildlife Management Area. But you can't get there because the wilds are across the swamp opening. However, the last mile of Long Island Sound beachfront is managed by the Milford branch of the Connecticut Audubon, which allows night fishing along with a key to their locked gate. Locals acquire memberships and keys by joining the Audubon. It is the only way to deal with the stringent parking maintained by local restrictions. Even when accessed properly, it is still a 20-minute walk to the good fishing.

Two spots dominate this location: Milford Point itself, which is most seaward; and the spur about 1,000 feet northwest, upriver, facing the swampy island. Both tides are good, but I give the drop an edge. Everybody either plugs or fly fishes here after dark.

DARBY DAM

Another local aspect of the Housatonic River is to fish at the dam in Darby where there is public parking. But that far upstream the entire character, while it is still brackish, changes to a mixed bag of both fresh- and saltwater species. Season depending, the hot periods are spring and fall for stripers up to 30 pounds, with an iffy winter-over fishery. Under the dam they get largemouth bass, white and yellow perch, sea-run trout that apparently washed down from a robust catch-and-release management upriver, and even an occasional Atlantic salmon. When fishing is good there can be some pretty wild collections of anglers that—depending upon your attitude— qualifies as group sport. A freshwater fishing license is needed north or upstream of the Wilbur Cross/Merritt Parkway (Route 15).

We rate this hot spot as a one star because of the access limitations and hassle related to Audubon memberships. But the fishing is considerably better than that or it would not be in this book.

CONTACT TIP: Call Stratford Bait and Tackle and ask for Chris or Chick if you want the word on Housey fishing, (203) 377-8091.

6
Silver Sands State Park (Charles Island)
Milford, Connecticut

BEST MONTHS TO FISH: May through November.
RECOMMENDED METHODS: Fly fishing, swimming plugs, and cut baits.
FISH YOU CAN EXPECT TO CATCH: Stripers and bluefish.
HOW TO GET THERE: From I–95, take exit 35, Schoolhouse Road south. Turn right onto Route 1 (Bridgeport Avenue), then left onto Meadows End Road. Follow Meadows End straight onto Pumpkin Delight Road. At the end of this road, turn right onto Monroe Street, then left onto Nettleton. Turn left at the barricade onto the park service road and follow it to the end. (Access will be changing, as this park is presently under development, and it still is unclear how roads will be managed.)

The major attraction of this hot spot is a ½-mile bar that connects with Charles Island. Wader-clad regulars like to work the rips that form between the island and shore, but access to the island is only possible at low tide, and it is necessary for anyone who goes there

Long Island Sound offers protected hot spots for stripers and blues.

to keep in mind the potential for being trapped. Because surf fishing is best done at night, it is mandatory that anyone doing any wading here be certain about tide, visibility, and direction. Until you are completely familiar with the area, be especially cautious.

No doubt other species can be taken here, but the targets are stripers and blues, and artificials dominate the methods. Silver Sands is not for everybody. On the other hand, if you know the striper ropes, this is a place worthy of finely tuned attentions. Swimming plugs tied direct—not encumbered with a wire leader—work well on slurping stripers. Fly fishermen should plan to use floating lines and the usual streamer patterns. Good spot.

CONTACT TIP: For more information on Silver Sands and other local spots, call Stratford Bait and Tackle, (203) 377-8091.

7
Enfield Dam, Connecticut River
Suffield, Connecticut

BEST MONTHS TO FISH: Late April to late June.

RECOMMENDED METHODS: Alewife simulating lures and big swimming plugs.

FISH YOU CAN EXPECT TO CATCH: Stripers.

HOW TO GET THERE: From I–91 take exit 47B to Route 190 west. After crossing the river, take Route 159 south, then take the first left onto Canal Street.

Another herring run fishery that is highly seasonal, Enfield Dam reflects population trends of both indigenous bait and stripers. Each spring linesides follow alewives and white shad up from the Sound to the eroding dam where both mill about. Without bait there are no stripers.

While anglers line up on both banks to toss baits and plugs, the west bank has the edge because of two nearby holes, better flow characteristics, and the availability of parking at Old Canal Park. Dependent upon snowmelt, spring water levels can be highly variable: One day fishermen can wade far out into the river among the rocks; another day the river roars white, nearly burying the dam. With such conditions there is some hazard to the river. Drownings take place every year although most victims are from boats. While examining conditions, it is good to keep in mind that water temperatures, which trigger the runs of both bait and gamefish, are more suitable when the water is low because snowmelt is colder. Otherwise, the later in the season, the better and bigger the bass run. As with the rest of the Striper Coast, small fish arrive first, more in April, and the cows become numerous in late May. Look for a top fish in the low forties and a predominance of smaller linesides. Naturally, the river will mirror coastwide population trends.

You may have to fish heavy tackle more to deal with the current and crowds. Locals can often be seen carrying two rods—a light 6-footer for snagging baits and a meat stick for the actual fishing. Here, a freshwater fishing license is required despite its tidewater status.

CONTACT TIP: To inquire about Enfield Dam, call Connecticut Outfitters, (860) 296-0110.

8
Hammonasset Beach State Park
Madison, Connecticut

BEST MONTHS TO FISH: May through November.
RECOMMENDED METHODS: Sea worms, chunk baits (bunker and mackerel), live eels, poppers, and big swimmers.
FISH YOU CAN EXPECT TO CATCH: Stripers and bluefish.
HOW TO GET THERE: From I–95 take exit 62, then follow the signs to the park.

The rock jetty at Meigs Point attracts the majority of angling attention within Hammonasset Beach State Park. Bottom fishermen tend to gather here in large crowds during seasonal peaks and weekends. (Fishing is limited to the jetty during the summer season.) The waters at the very end of the jetty are most popular because of the depth there. By fall, particularly after dark—a time when the best fishing of the year is available—this spot is pure solitude. The entire beach is open after Labor Day, and it is not uncommon for great schools of bluefish to be seen within casting distance. Park personnel issue permits for fishing after closing time so that anglers can drive their cars from the entrance gate to the beach.

Madison's Stu Jones, winner of the 1994 Massachusetts Governor's Cup with a 57-pounder, likes Meigs Point. "I like the flood better than the ebb here because of how the rip makes up with the jetty," said Jones. "During falling water your eel or plug has to go through rocks that are fouled with old tackle and lines that are caught there. But during the rise the current flow is northwest and the rip line sets up right at your feet. I flip eels underhand back at the submerged rocks, drifting them through the rip like garden worms for trout. I have been pretty successful."

CONTACT TIP: Antlers and Anglers, (860) 245-1007, can advise you on Meigs Point fishing.

9
Cornfield Point
Old Saybrook, Connecticut

BEST MONTHS TO FISH: May through November (but skip August).
RECOMMENDED METHODS: Plugs, eels, fly fishing, chunks, and crabs.
FISH YOU CAN EXPECT TO CATCH: Stripers, bluefish, and blackfish.
HOW TO GET THERE: From I–95 take exit 67 onto Route 1 south, take a left at the light onto Route 154 south, follow to a left turn onto Cornfield Point Road, and continue to land's end.

Connecticut shores are commonly fly fished.

All of this rocky shoreline is productive, but the fishing improves as one makes one's way west to the point. Watch for evidence of moving water, which is more likely down to the right. Big swimming plugs are popular here as are live eels, but because of the rocks, eel retrieve speeds should be slightly faster to keep them from getting lost. Fly fishers like the sand flats to the north. You can also access these flats from the Old Saybrook Town Beach, although public access is often restricted in the summer.

As in any other southwest-facing location, winds from that quarter improve things; however, a strong southeaster, usually an indication of an impending storm, also makes the interaction of the currents better. Starting in early October, there is a great fall run of good-sized blackfish that take green or hermit crabs like candy.

This is a popular local spot with fragile access considerations. Some anglers park at the rear of the Castle Inn lot, but officials tell me that it is illegal to do so and that your car may be towed. Yes, parking is a problem.

CONTACT TIP: River's End Tackle, (860) 388-2283, knows Cornfield Point and more.

10
Connecticut Department of Environmental Protection Marine Headquarters
Old Lyme, Connecticut

BEST MONTHS TO FISH: March through December.

RECOMMENDED METHODS: Baits or lures, depending on the species, and fly fishing.

FISH YOU CAN EXPECT TO CATCH: Stripers, bluefish, and blackfish.

HOW TO GET THERE: Take exit 70 from I–95 to Route 156 north; then take a right onto Ferry Road and continue to land's end. There will be signs.

A fishing pier, completed in the spring of '93, extends from the south end of the state property (beneath the Old Lyme railroad bridge) to the mouth of the Lieutenant River—a fly-fishing mecca. This one earns hot-spot status because it is highly accessible and productive on account of its placement on the Connecticut River—hardly a risky call. Open twenty-four hours a day, it is intended to be the answer to the problems that so often bedevil shore fishing. Fly fishers leave the end of the pier and wade the bars in the deep night with floating lines. Patterns are dressed to imitate river shiners, sperling and—some years—baby bunker.

CONTACT TIP: Information for this area and other spots is available from River's End Tackle, (860) 388-2283.

11
Sound View Beach
Old Lyme, Connecticut

BEST MONTHS TO FISH: May, June, October, and November.
RECOMMENDED METHODS: Plugs, live or rigged eels, and fly fishing.
FISH YOU CAN EXPECT TO CATCH: Stripers and blues.
HOW TO GET THERE: From I–95 take exit 71 onto Four Mile River Road. Take a right on Route 156 at the stop sign, then a left onto Hartford Avenue and follow to the end. Parking is limited and at your own risk.

Two major areas of structure on this sandy, gently sloping beach should be tested first. About 300 yards west of the parking lot, there is a small rocky point that is popular two hours either side of high tide. Outside those hours, efforts should be cursory, and I'm told that the sand before that is a waste of time.

The other spot, Griswold Point, is about a mile west and just about as far as many of us are willing to walk. Matt Zajac, a competent river guide and regular, however, tells me that it is Connecticut's answer to the Cape's old-time Chatham Inlet, only smaller—and well worth the effort. The reason for this is that currents from the Blackhall and Connecticut rivers collide with Long Island Sound to create a garland of moving water, bait, stripers, and blues. Here, juvenile herring and menhaden emigrate from the nearby Connecticut River in late summer and fall (mature spawning baitfish earlier). Onshore sou'west winds stir it up for better fishing, and nor'westers cause the Connecticut River water to move better. Casting from shore, you can reach a depth of 13 feet. There is excellent fishing all through the dropping tide here, so try it after having worked the aforementioned rocky outcropping at high tide. While all methods work, this is dreamland for fly fishers. Possibly the best-in-state!

CONTACT TIP: Information central for this region is River's End Tackle (860) 388-2283, across the river in Old Saybrook, where Pat Abate knows what is happening and where, as well as what you'll need.

12
Niantic River
Niantic, Connecticut

BEST MONTHS TO FISH: May through November.

RECOMMENDED METHODS: Bunkers, herring, bucktail jigs, live eels, and fly fishing.

FISH YOU CAN EXPECT TO CATCH: Stripers and bluefish.

HOW TO GET THERE: For the western shore, take exit 74 from I–95, to Route 161 toward Niantic, then make a left at the light onto Route 156. Either take the left road before the Niantic River Drawbridge and follow to the end, or take a left immediately after the drawbridge, then a left at the stop sign. Safe parking on the west, or Niantic, side of the river is limited to the access ramp on the north side of the road. Eastern shore access is from Route 156, Rope Ferry Road; at the traffic light, turn north onto Niantic River Road, take the first left onto B Street, turn left onto Fourth Street, and take the first right onto Rope Ferry Road to public parking at the end.

Fishing is done from the railroad bridge at the mouth of the Niantic River. To the south, or seaward of the railroad track, you can fish both sides of the river. There is also good fishing on the west bank between the bridges. Beaches on both sides of the river mouth produce good fishing, with the eastern shore having an edge.

When there are bunker in the river—and thus the opportunity to snag fresh baits—it is possible to feed one from this bridge and do very well with both stripers and blues. At times, there have been some moby blues taken here in this way. Currents from this river bridge are too powerful for bottom fishing, and plugging, except at slack tide, is not a viable alternative. But a bucktail jig, for those who use them well and allow them to drift deep, can be used for stripers in the night if there are no fresh baits available. Best water is during the drop in tide. Pat Abate, a local regular with a coastwide reputation, told me that about twenty years ago there was a striper taken here that weighed in the mid-sixties. Not too shabby. Eddies or slack tides in which you can hold bottom produce some decent blackfish. It is possible to fish bottom on the south side of the inlet. Also, some surfcasters like to fish live eels by casting and retrieving slowly.

Just about any bait found coastwide is represented here and thus can be used with delivery methods dictated by the motion of the water. Anglers have been known to lament the oft-repeated complaint that bass will show up in the Niantic—usually in the deep of night—slashing and slurping but not taking any baits or artificials. Abate says that this happens when the squid are abundant, but it may also occur during June worm hatches, which have driven otherwise calm people stark raving mad. South of the inlet, particularly on the outgoing tide, when bait is being swept past, the action can be better than in the inlet. That is one reason why it is a popular fly-fishing spot.

CONTACT TIP: Hillyers Tackle Shop, (860) 443-7615, knows what is happening on the Niantic River.

Bluefish are targets of opportunity, especially during summer months.

13
Harkness Memorial State Park
Waterford, Connecticut

BEST MONTHS TO FISH: May through November, though August is slow.

RECOMMENDED METHODS: Plugs, cut baits, eels, hermit crabs, and fly fishing.

FISH YOU CAN EXPECT TO CATCH: Stripers, bluefish, blackfish, and some fluke.

HOW TO GET THERE: From I–95, take exit 75 on to Route 1 east and drive four miles to a right turn.

Best fishing is west (to the right) of this rocky, curving shoreline. The boulder-strewn shore offers plenty of attractive hiding places for good-sized stripers. There is also a reef within casting distance that no doubt draws some linesides to the area.

Some Harkness regulars will come equipped to fish cut bait (menhaden or mackerel) but have a supply of plugs in the bag—swimmers at night and poppers by day—for when they see or hear fish working. Of course, when things are known to be good, surf fishers will come with live eels. While stripers are what most are seeking, bluefish often end up as targets of opportunity. With all the rocks, this is also a great blackfish spot starting in early October. Use green or hermit crabs with a bank sinker on the bottom. The sandy shallow areas near Goshen Cove are popular with fly fishers who use floating lines.

Best fishing time for all methods is two hours either side of high tide, particularly when this period matches up with dawn or dusk. No parking hassles.

CONTACT TIP: River's End Tackle, (860) 388-2283.

14
Thames River
Norwich, Connecticut

BEST MONTHS TO FISH FOR STRIPERS: November through March.

RECOMMENDED METHODS: Small lures like jigs and Super Fluke, some bottom baits.

FISH YOU CAN EXPECT TO CATCH: Winter-over stripers, blues in the summer.

HOW TO GET THERE: More a region than a particular spot, from Route 395 take exit 80 east into Norwich.

The qualifying aspect of the Thames River for this book is that it is one of those rare winter-over fisheries not all that common on the Striper Coast. A moderate migratory population of stripers returns to the Norwich area every winter providing angling opportunity for boat and shore fishermen. No one knows why this winter fishery has evolved, because the warm water discharge once believed to draw winter fish has become less reliable with the decommissioning of the old Montville Power Plant that once reliably produced a robust warm water discharge. There is a new power plant but surprisingly the fishing does not always take place right at the occasional warm water outflow. The conditions producing the best fishing remain a sort of a mystery where is it not as simple as finding the plant in power production by watching the steam and smoke from its stacks. At times the west bank of the Thames downstream and south of the the plant is a suitable shore fishing location but the stripers are often on the move even when water is mid-winter cold.

Just as many shore fish are taken from the Norwich docks right in town. While this upstream location remains tidal, there is less reliance on tide in this fishery than might be found elsewhere. There has been considerable loss of access to the river over the years but state-owned and -managed Fort Shantock State Park in Montville (off Route 32 north of the Pequot Bridge) is open for fishing and located in the prime parts of the river. The Norwich Marina and dock right in Norwich is commonly bait fished on the bottom. Time was when fresh herring or alewives were the ticket, but recent restrictions on their use to protect these baitfish have banned that. If alewife populations ever recover, they could again be a viable bait choice.

Use of artificials works best if on the small side and running deep as stripers tend to stack on the bottom. Forget poppers. The old-time MirrOLures your uncle used have largely been replaced with the plethora of modern deep running rubber shads. Super Flukes were in the limelight at the time of this writing but fishing being what it is, that could change quickly. It is safe to say that whatever works elsewhere will have its day on the Thames. Drastic changes in temperatures are thought to enhance the fishing.

The best lineside you'll ever see here would not weigh over 30 pounds with the average more like five pounds. There was a 57-pounder taken in the region years ago but I wouldn't count on that happening again. Heavy breathers of the Striper Coast lust over this spot more because of the off-season opportunity it provides. And that might just be the injustice in the reputation of the place. Spring runs of alewives, with their striper-drawing scent, provide a great spring run of new fish after winter-overs have left, sustaining activity well into June. Anglers gather at the Shetucket River Dam in spring to cash in on new fish drawn upriver by the alewife run. There is also a lot of activity behind the football field on the Shetucket's east bank along Route 165 more because of public access. November stripers pour in while suitable water temperatures encourage their feeding. Schools of bunker, vast many summer seasons, will draw bluefish during what some might call the "off months."

Gales Ferry (take Route 12 to Stoddard Wharf Road), according to the Division of Marine Fisheries, is a famous summer hot spot for both bass and blues. The river makes a bend here and the main channel comes within casting range of the riverbank. Menhaden are the forage base that are chunked on the bottom but the gang uses swimmers and poppers during this warm weather fishing period.

A freshwater fishing license is required in the whole area in spite of there being so much salt in the grog. Connecticut policy for setting the line for license requirement varies from river to river. We've found it necessary to lower the rating of this hot spot due to reduced access, and a reputation for boat fishing that is greater than that of the shore.

CONTACT TIP: Call the Fish Connection on Route 12 in Preston, (860) 885-1739.

15
Bluff Point State Park
Groton, Connecticut

BEST MONTHS TO FISH: April through November.

RECOMMENDED METHODS: Plugs or baits, depending on the species.

FISH YOU CAN EXPECT TO CATCH: Stripers, bluefish, blackfish, scup, and winter flounder.

HOW TO GET THERE: Take exit 88 from I–95 to Route 117 south. Take a right on Route 1, then a left at the traffic light onto Depot Road, and follow it to the end under the railroad tracks and into the park.

The rocky shoreline at Bluff Point is about ¾ mile from the parking lot. Striperwise, things don't get going here until June, but they hold well into November; expect blues from July into November. All the methods—cut baits and plugs—that work elsewhere are utilized here. Among the rockier areas, expect some blackfish (tautog) in late April. The best bait then is a sea worm on the bottom with a bank sinker. For scup (porgies), fish the sandy areas with freshwater-sized light tackle using a fingernail-sized sliver of squid or a small section of broken sea worm with a trout hook. The first scup appear in June, and they become more numerous as summer goes on.

Poquonock Cove, which is off to the west in the park, and closer, is a good spot for winter flounder in early spring on the flood tide. Use sea worms and the same small hooks.

CONTACT TIP: Fish Connection, (860) 885-1739, will tell you about Bluff Point fishing.

RHODE ISLAND

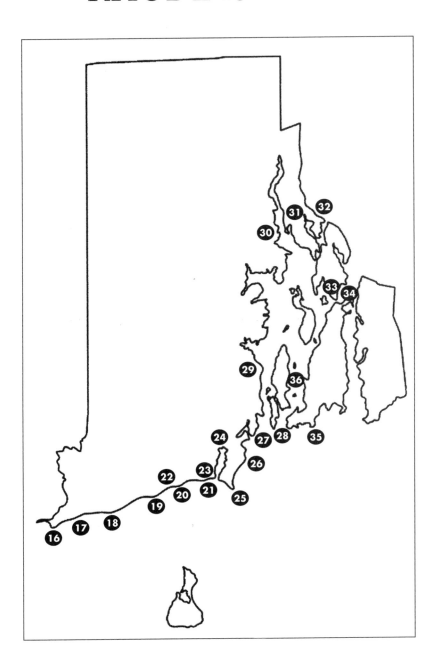

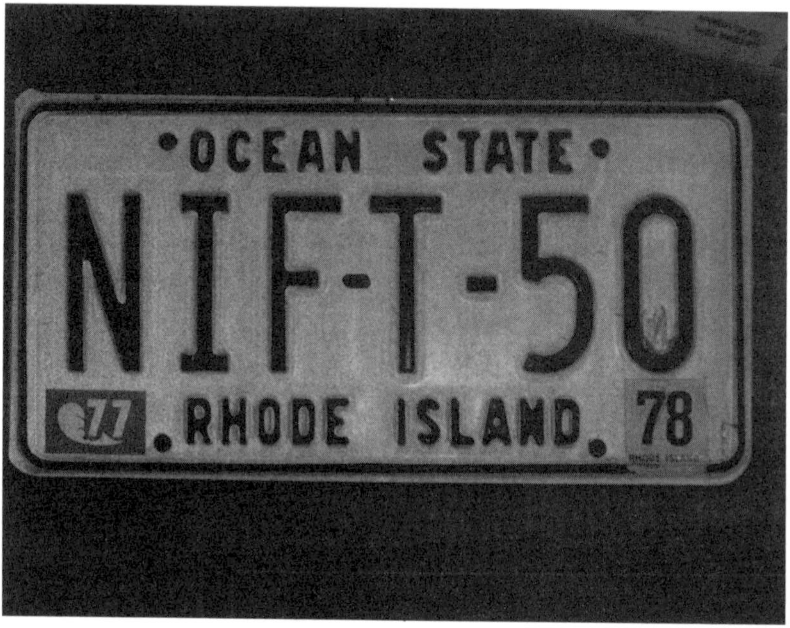
OCEAN STATE
NIFT-T-50
77
RHODE ISLAND
78

Rhode Island

It might sound great on paper to read that this little state has a 400-mile coastline, but that is another one of those nook-and-cranny measurements. The truth is that the Ocean State can be divided into two sections: the south shore beaches (about 20 miles), and the area related to Narragansett Bay. The beaches are pristine, and the waters off Narragansett and Newport, both rockbound shorelines without comparison for natural beauty, are said to be so clear that they are favored by divers. Sad to say, deep into Narragansett Bay, the water is severely polluted. Still, gamefish are not deterred from going inland, clear to Providence, and the bay affords some protection from sea storms.

Coastal policies are favorable to fishing, and Rhode Islanders love the natural opportunities the sea provides. Still, as has been the case in areas to the south, there is some overpossessive behavior, a lot of it (but not all) from visitors. As elsewhere, there have been battles over beach access, and courts have ruled that a landowner's control ends at "mean high tide." Among Rhode Island's ever-lengthening list of scandals, there has been an expensive rights-of-way study that showed that people abutting such rights-of-way have long hidden them with a little ivy, stone, and mortar to cover and hide the public's access to the shore. Worse, signs that were meant to inform the public have repeatedly been taken down to prevent encouragement of their use. But my home state's failings seem worse because I am familiar with them, not because people here abuse the public's right of access more than elsewhere. We who love a place are often the harshest critics.

Still, it is a good place to fish, in that it affords the shore fisherman a hundred times the opportunity of any place this side of New York. It is the beginning of access opportunities that have been sorely missed since mid–New Jersey. I can say this with some comfort when examining those spots that failed to make the cut.

Upper Narragansett Bay has a number of locally popular spots that have their nights. Sandy Point, Conimicut Point, Warwick Light—to name but a few—yield stripers in spring and bluefish on summer nights when menhaden are available; yet it would be a violation of my mission if I were to elaborate any further upon them: not because they are secrets, but because they are of only local significance. Barrington Beach fell short by a slight margin; some hot spots are tough calls.

There is another group of nearly suitable spots on the east bank of Narragansett Bay that, while they don't rate inclusion here, could provide some worthy shore fishing opportunities. Stifled access to the opening of Tiverton's Nannaquaket Pond requires a commando raid to access it for the fishing but the outflow has bass during the outgoing tide. Further south on the Sakonnet River, the Seapowet March Wildlife Management Area is publicly accessible but the outflow is small and any such place where water comes from a productive marsh that sponsors marine life is going to draw gamefish.

Similarly, the outflow of fresh water from Nonquit Pond holds bass but it is a case of access and parking.

The great salt ponds that open only occasionally can produce wildly productive activity, especially if the herring are running. We have that with Briggs Marsh and Quicksand Pond in Little Compton but the openings are unreliable, difficult to access and nearly impossible to time. We want the spots in this book to be more forgiving than that. Now let's go to the places we can use.

16
Napatree Point
Westerly, Rhode Island

BEST MONTHS TO FISH: May, June, October, and November.
RECOMMENDED METHODS: Plugging, live eels, and fly fishing.
FISH YOU CAN EXPECT TO CATCH: Stripers, bluefish, fluke, porgies, and bonito.
HOW TO GET THERE: From Westerly, take Route 1A south; then pick up Watch Hill Road at Avondale. Take a right into the parking lot at land's end.

Guarding the east edge of the opening to Little Narragansett Bay, Napatree Point is a 1¼-mile barrier beach of generally sandy shore that ends in a rocky point. While you can find bass or blues anywhere along this stretch, the rocky point is the most reliable spot on account of the rips that form here and on offshore reefs. Where the sand meets the rocks is a good location during the ebbing tide, which flows right to left. On this seaward side, wind from any southern quadrant will cause the surf to collide with currents if the tide is dropping. On the incoming tide, fish any of the rocky shoreline to the right. When the tide is rising, the wind can combine with these currents to form a better rip. Don't overlook the eddy on the inside edge in the back. "The Naps" are a popular fly-fishing spot, particularly on a north-side mussel bar. The walk out is an invigorating ramble in the majesty of a Rhode Island sunset.

I omit the summer months from this hot-spot listing because of parking problems. During the bathing season, night access is difficult and day access just about impossible.

CONTACT TIP: From Watch Hill to Quonnie, call Captain Don's Bait and Tackle, (401) 322-0544, for fishing information.

17

Watch Hill
Westerly, Rhode Island

BEST MONTHS TO FISH: October and November.

RECOMMENDED METHODS: Plugging.

FISH YOU CAN EXPECT TO CATCH: Stripers and bluefish.

HOW TO GET THERE: From Westerly, take Route 1A south, then pick up Watch Hill Road at Avondale. Follow the signs to Watch Hill Light.

Watch Hill Light, a Coast Guard station, has limited parking facilities that are restricted to authorized vehicles. It is best, therefore, to park in the lot at Watch Hill across from the carousel and walk the quarter mile out. This rocky peninsula is a natural obstruction for passing gamefish, which have to go around it. A natural spot for plugging, with its open water surf, Watch Hill Light is usually fished at the crack of dawn or at sunset. It is especially popular during the fall migration. Traditionally, the best side is the east, a rocky place where casters often position themselves on a prominent stone, risking getting dumped off by a pushy sea. Like all coastal stones, they can also be slippery.

Those with an over-sand vehicle can access the light from the east by driving the 2 miles of beach that are open during the fall. Entry is gained from Misquamicut. At the corner, where the sand beach meets the rocks of the light, I have seen stripers and blues packed in during a raging, prestorm southeast wind, when the surf was white with foam and the only thing breaking the coloration was the green and dark backs of stripers and blues. I hasten to add that the 2-mile stretch of beach itself can provide angling opportunities for both lure and bait anglers, as the bottom here is sandy and free of obstruction. In some years, the outer bar structure here is as good as that of Misquamicut, to the east. Incidentally, do not try to fish in front of private property at Misquamicut Beach during the summer.

CONTACT TIP: Information is available from Captain Don's Bait and Tackle, (401) 322-0544.

18
Weekapaug Breachway
Westerly, Rhode Island

BEST MONTHS TO FISH: October and November.

RECOMMENDED METHODS: Plugging and fly fishing.

FISH YOU CAN EXPECT TO CATCH: Stripers and bluefish, occasional tunoids.

HOW TO GET THERE: Follow signs from Shore Road (Route 1A) south to Weekapaug, or turn south on Dunn's Corner Road.

Winnapaug Pond is a natural estuary that provides a haven and breeding ground for baitfish that appeal to stripers. There is a constant flow that fills and drains this pond through the opening of Weekapaug Breachway, which is flanked by a pair of rocky jetties. During a dropping tide, you can see the lines of infusion as currents of the estuary reach seaward. Naturally, the shallow waters of the pond are heated by day, and in autumn they are cooled at night. No doubt these variations in temperature, along with the scent of bait, exert some influence over passing gamefish. As a result, the opening at the end of the two jetties is a popular spot for surfcasters. A good method is to drift live eels seaward with the current. That is easy here because of the smooth, sandy bottom. Moreover, with a road bridge only a few hundred yards upstream, one can park on either side to fish from whichever jetty suits one's fancy.

CONTACT TIP: Information is available from Captain Don's Bait and Tackle, (401) 322-0544.

19

Quonochontaug Breachway
Charlestown, Rhode Island

BEST MONTHS TO FISH: May through November.

RECOMMENDED METHODS: Plugging, jigs, live eels, and fly fishing.

FISH YOU CAN EXPECT TO CATCH: Stripers, bluefish, and occasional bonito.

HOW TO GET THERE: For the west bank: Follow the shore road east from Weekapaug. The oversand route is private, but the Rhode Island Mobile Sports (RIMS) fishermen honor members of other beach buggy associations. Nights or off-season, you can park at the beginning behind the dunes and walk the beach for good fishing. For the east bank: Just east of the intersection of Route 216 and Route 1, take a south turn onto West Beach Road and follow it around a circle to the west until it ends at a public boat-launching ramp.

*Rhody jetties
are famously
productive.*

"Quonnie," as it is so fondly known by regulars, is the first of a number of classic striper hot spots that deserve special treatment. I say this because this hot spot has its own legion of rabid followers who will no doubt be retching in the dunes when they see their favorite spot in these pages. And the reason is: Quonnie has everything.

The breachway, which is an inlet flanked by jetties, leads to a clean back-pond estuary. Moreover, the passage to Quonochontaug Pond is both short enough and straight enough to permit an exchange of water of sufficient force to keep the inlet from silting over or slowing down. The key to this spot is the power of these tidal exchanges, because during the drop, Quonnie Pond water reaches far to seaward, tolling in forage and gamefish. My guess is that the gallonage here is double that of the aforementioned Weekapaug Breachway.

Of course, these dropping currents produce the top striper fishing opportunities in the region. At the seaward end of the jetties, surf fishers cast across current, then free spool swimming plugs seaward until their spools are depleted. Then they let their plugs swing under tension through the flow and pause in the eddy, following with a slow retrieve. Works easy. At the early part of the first outward flow, many surfcasters will fish the east jetty; however, this is not a good spot once the tide is down some, because the shallows of that bank often cause plugs to hang up on rocks. Moreover, I have seen some good fish lost in these rocks. Access is from West Beach Road, off Route 1. Use your head parking and keep in mind that local cottage owners notice less in the deep of night and in the off-season.

The west bank is the best side for drifting a plug in the dropping tide. Access, however, presents certain challenges—and this is no accident. First, it is 1½ miles down the beach, which is best covered with a four-wheeler; second, no beach driving is allowed in Rhode Island without a Coastal Resources Management Beach Permit issued at nearby Burlingame State Park on the north side of Route 1 in Charlestown; third, this is a private, residents-only beach. What can work either for or against you is that RIMS members are counted as landowners there. This means that each member has access rights to Quonnie, and they are permitted to have guests. Thus, if you can take the right people to dinner, barter some choice tin squids, or offer help at some other time and territory, you just might be able to fish there. Membership in United Mobile Sportsfishermen is honored. And there are other ways.

The same road you would use for the east bank (West Beach Road) also leads to state land in the back where the breachway opens to the pond. Here you'll find a public boat-launching ramp and free parking with virtually no restrictions except for camping. It is an easy matter to cross with a float tube, canoe, or other marginal craft, and after a short walk to the front (less than half a mile), it is possible to fish from state property without trespassing. People who kayak the pond can launch here.

A great deal is made of the seaward end of Quonnie Breachway on the dropping tide. It is one of those local traditions that is pretty hard to dispute. You can't argue with all that history. Also, there is a certain esoteric group of hard-core regulars who dearly love meeting on the rocks to drift plugs, gab, knock down a beer or two, and otherwise celebrate the glory of surfcasting.

The rise in tide, particularly if fish have been showing on the drop, can compensate for a slight loss of bass with a great increase in solitude. Five fish that are all yours are better than a hundred shared with thirty other casters. With water coming in—hurrying to the back pond with the will of seamen on liberty—it is possible to drift heavy bucktail jigs all through the opening. Landing, however, is the problem. Even big fish, after fighting the current when heading to the open sea, will eventually drop back into the breachway. To land them, you will have to deal with the rocky banks. Unlike your counterpart fishing the dropping tide who can beach a monster, you will have to climb down slippery rocks amid often vicious currents.

But now for Quonnie's easier part: in the back, where the jetties end and the back estuary begins, it is possible to drive the family auto (as mentioned earlier) to the east side. Here, walking north on the flats in waders, a shore fisherman can enjoy the quiet, protected, estuarine nature of Quonnie Pond. It is a perfect spot for light spinning tackle with smaller plugs. Or, where better to fly fish than among shallows, where sperling skitter across the surface while pursued by hungry linesides? No police hassles, no crowds; your worst disturbance is likely to be teenage "parkers" who might not understand the importance of discreet headlights. Also, never overlook the breachway itself, as you will often find some moby linesides hanging out in the currents there. If the quiet and deep night mood of the back has one failing, it is that it can lull you into a false sense of comfort, so that you will not be ready when Mr. Big comes along. It happens all the time.

CONTACT TIP: Information is available from Captain Don's Bait and Tackle, (401) 322-0544.

Blitz fishing is common on the South Shore.

20
East Beach
Charlestown, Rhode Island

BEST MONTHS TO FISH: June through November.
RECOMMENDED METHODS: Plugging, live eels, and bottom baits.

FISH YOU CAN EXPECT TO CATCH: Stripers, bluefish, blackfish, weakfish, flounder, and porgy.

HOW TO GET THERE: Access is south from Route 1 on East Beach Road, the first right after the fire station. (Over-sand vehicle recommended.)

I have a love/hate relationship with East Beach. On the "hate" side: deep water and invisible structure make it a poor spot for the practice of reading the beach. Every yard of this shore, and I have fished every one, feels no different than any other. Two notable exceptions are "The Mound," roughly 3 miles east of the beach access, where there is an ocean current, and a stretch west of the breachway where you can sometimes feel cobblestones on the bottom. I have felt them many times, but only after a diver told me about them. Also, about 200 yards to the west of the breachway lies "Split Rock"—a pair of rocks usually at casting distance—which has ocean current flowing by in which linesides sometimes hang out. Otherwise, it is a straight, lackluster beach with little for a beach reader to sink his or her teeth into. Now to the parts I love.

It is all sand—no wrecks or anything that will damage a line. The breachway's jetty acts as a stopping point where bait is often trapped. A similar situation occurs 4 miles to the west, at Fresh Pond Rocks. Stripers, and certainly blues, can be anywhere along the beach. Moreover, at the base of the angle of the beach, there is a place called "The Rut," where there is a small drop-off of 6 to 12 inches caused by the erosive action of the surf. I have hooked many moby stripers so close to the beach—all hanging out at "The Rut"—that I could easily have lifted my eel out of the water before they took it.

I have also come upon schools of stripers while plugging or eel fishing. All methods work here, and I have seen anglers sitting on their tailgates in fall, watching lines baited with squid, chunks, or sea worms. The daylight panfishing here is about as good as it gets. It is possible to sweeten a hook with a tiny ribbon of squid or a ½-inch section of sea worm and feel drumming and tapping the whole time you are fishing—and filling a bucket with delectable 10-inch porgy. I have caught a variety of fish here, including blackfish, weakfish, flounder, and even kingfish. This assortment of fish that appear here in varying levels each July and August should remind us that all marine populations are highly cyclical. Weakfish, for example, at this point in their cycle, are not to be found except in limited numbers in the mid-Atlantic states. Summer flounder and scup are all over the coast in numbers that make you feel that the bottom must be lined with them. I can recall times when, during the November migration, we inadvertently caught stripers, blues, weakfish, and cod on the same lures, although opportunities for cod from the beach are unreliable most years.

Naturally, the fall migration elevates the popularity of East Beach, particularly in early November. There have been few fall seasons when, driving the beach at night, stopping periodically along the way, I didn't find stripers, or blues, or both. One reason for the reliability of this spot is that over-sand vehicles are permitted on the 4 miles of productive beach. The ability to drive the beach introduces an element of efficiency to your efforts that is not possible elsewhere on this section of coast until you reach the Cape.

One note, though, concerning driving on East Beach: because this shore is one of those fragile ecosystems that hang in the balance and could be denied to surfcasters by the carelessness of just one driver, religious observance of the rules is necessary for the continued access of this fine stretch of shoreline. If the wheel of your vehicle kills so much as one tuft of beach grass, or a single plant of beach plums, you are finished with driving the beach—and the fines are severe. If it happens with any frequency, we are all finished! Stay on the trails. Stay off the dunes.

Two usage types are available, according to the season: front beach, for the period September 15 through April 15; and back trail, for the rest of the year. Keep in mind that all regulations are subject to change, and this book cannot serve as legal justification for any behavior. Any departure from where you are supposed to be at a given season, or from the regulations as they stand, is reason for revocation of the permit.

No doubt the rest of Rhode Island's south shore offers similar fishing opportunities, but utilization of a beach vehicle is not permitted on the stretch that includes Green Hill and parts of Matunuck except for a brief period in fall. This gives East Beach an undeniable advantage.

CONTACT TIP: For information call Breachway Bait and Tackle, (401) 364-6407.

21
Charlestown Breachway
Charlestown, Rhode Island

BEST MONTHS TO FISH: May through November.

RECOMMENDED METHODS: Plugs, bucktail jigs, live eels, and fly fishing.

FISH YOU CAN EXPECT TO CATCH: Stripers, bluefish, bonito, and blackfish.

HOW TO GET THERE: Follow the signs to Charlestown Breachway from Route 1 in Charlestown. There is a state-run parking area for anglers.

Charlestown Breachway is no secret. Still, the fishing is good.

Five miles east of Quonnie, you'll find a geographically similar situation in Charlestown. The main difference is that access to both sides of the flanking jetties is through public property. On the east bank, the state maintains a "Public Fishing Area" with two parking lots: One is for anglers' autos; the other is a self-contained area for camping vehicles. All east-bank access is on drivable road. The west jetty to Charlestown Breachway, on the other hand, is accessible by a 4-mile over-sand trail that requires four-wheel drive and a permit and is closely regulated.

The inlet here provides slightly less flow than that of Quonnie despite the fact that it serves a much larger estuarine pond. This is because the channel to the inside is narrow, shallow, and winding. Worse, with reduced flow, siltation tends to accelerate the closing of the channel. About every twenty years, give or take, the government has to come in and dredge the channel out to keep the back pond alive. If you are unfortunate enough to try this area when the channel is in need of dredging, you might be disappointed with Charlestown Breachway's fishing because of subdued currents.

As it is with Quonnie, drifting plugs on the outgoing tide is popular—only, in this case, it is the east jetty that enjoys the bulk of angling interest. There are three reasons for this: First, the east jetty is more accessible; second, during the falling tide, ocean currents moving east bend the seaward lines of infusion to an east hook that produces a favorable eddy; and, third, the regrettable bad positioning of "Plug Rock" on the west side makes the east jetty the clear choice. On either bank, however, there is deep water.

Placement of the stones and their later rearrangement by the forces of nature make the east jetty a lot wetter than the west. I have often stood on the west side on a night when the wind was heaving a murderous sea, and the east-side boys, walls of water raining down on them 20 feet back from the end, made you wish you could do something to relieve their suffering. Of course, being on the drier side was small compensation for the hazards of having Plug Rock a scant 20 yards downtide, which is covered with barnacles that can nick a line down to half its rated strength. And yet, the west side is usually better during a rising tide. I have seen moby linesides position themselves in the opening and around the end to face the current. Here it is possible to drift a live eel, plug the outside, or run a bucktail jig through the strongest currents. But again, I advise you to fight a fish that goes out against the current with all you can muster, because Plug Rock remains a hazard; it is the big fish that swim against the current when in trouble. I have paid their price. A common angling mistake here is to fish with gear that is too light.

A choice time to keep in mind is when the sea current changes to early rise while the breachway current is still falling; then, for about two hours, the hook, or eddy, will be on the west side, which favors that side. Another terrific period is slack tide, about three hours after high or low tide on the tide chart for this location, when all fish change positions for a better feeding opportunity. Tautog fishing—using little green crabs for bait—is easier at slack tide. Because this spot is flow dependent, moon tides (new and full) are best. If you happen to be around during a brisk southeast, that wind favors Charlestown for some reason. Keep in mind, however, that southeast is the wind that precedes storms.

The back of the breachway, all the way to the open back pond, can produce some surprisingly good fishing at times; however, boat traffic is heavy here and one would do best to explore in the deep of night during the week. Small fish are more likely here, but I really hesitate saying that, because the ocean is loaded with wild cards. Great fly fishing here.

CONTACT TIP: For information call Breachway Bait and Tackle, (401) 364-6407.

22
Green Hill Beach
Charlestown, Rhode Island

BEST MONTHS TO FISH: September, October, November.
RECOMMENDED METHODS: Any artificials, rigged or live eels.
FISH YOU CAN EXPECT TO CATCH: Stripers, blues, summer flounder.
HOW TO GET THERE: From Route 1 in Charlestown, take Matunuck School House Road east for 1½ miles to a right onto Charlestown Beach Road. After about a mile, you will see a town parking lot at a sharp right turn in the road. From there it is a short walk over the dunes to the shore.

Late-summer bluefish hang out at Green Hill Beach.

East of Charlestown Breachway, Green Hill Beach makes the list of hot spots by virtue of its proximity to the rest of the Rhode Island south shore. The stretch is about 1½ miles of straight, lackluster sand with virtually no structure, jetties, or identifiable alteration in the seascape. Still, you can't have a location bordered on each of its ends by other memorable hot spots without including it. This spot is easily accessible all season from the Charlestown Town Beach parking lot. Once on the front, you can walk the surf line east casting as you go. As with the rest of the shore front between Matunuck and Watch Hill, there is a rut right under the last wave where bass often follow only a rod length away from you.

But the glory of this location is the famous fall migration when beach-buggy jockeys are allowed to drive the beach after September 15th. Many is the regular who has come upon a bunch of gamefish busting on bait in the surf. That is not to say that all good fishing here is that visual. Indeed, it is possible to be fishing a quiet ho-hum night the way I was in 1966 when all hell breaks loose.

As a family we had gone there in a camper rig for the long Columbus Day weekend, a perfect time to run into fish headed south for the winter. On the route to the beach we checked one of the tackle shops and were told that fishing had been surprisingly slow and nobody was doing anything. There were few fishing and those in the area were in bed early. It did not look good. I sacked in setting my alarm for a pre-dawn try but I was not excited. The next morning I put a chunk on the bottom, and plugged with a second rod using a loaded Junior Atom plug that Bob Pond of Atom Manufacturing had given me. I was not excited but there was a crisp cool in the mid-October air so I just stood in the gentle surf casting the plug while eyeballing the bait rod. Not long after starting, I got this awful whack on the plug and began fighting a fish that headed east down the beach toward my bait rod. All I could think of was getting tangled with the other stick. Consequently, I had to decide whether to go over the other line or under. I took a chance and went over and got lucky. After a while the brute fish was finning in the first wave, slowing down in its effort to escape. I knew it was big and hoped the gentle surf would help in getting it in. When a good wave broke, I pressured the monster but it stayed outside. Another wave and I tried again, only this time it popped out of the outside, sliding up onto the wet sand where I could keep up a slight pressure to keep it from sliding back down the hill into escape water. As I reached for its gills, I heard a tinkle of metallic noise from my plug falling off but I had the bugger and held on while a wave washed us both. It was a 51-pound striper and it carved my appreciation for Green Hill in stone. I love that place.

CONTACT TIP: Breachway Bait and Tackle, (401) 364-6407.

23
Deep Hole
Matunuck, Rhode Island

BEST MONTHS TO FISH: April, May, October, and November.

RECOMMENDED METHODS: Lures and fly fishing.

FISH YOU CAN EXPECT TO CATCH: Stripers, bluefish, and fluke.

HOW TO GET THERE: There are two accesses to this area: Deep Hole proper is approached from the south side of Route 1 on Matunuck Beach Road. For the east end of Matunuck go south, or right, from Route 1 by using Succotash Road from U.S. 1 to find East Matunuck State Beach and the West Wall.

The most dramatic alteration in the otherwise straight structure running east of Charlestown Breachway lies in Matunuck. Starting with Carpenter's Bar, which is so shallow that it is largely exposed at low tide, there are a number of worthwhile natural structures that appeal to stripers. Many striper regulars will gather at Carpenter's during the tail end of the drop and will endure, if there is any action, until rising water drives them off the bar. Carpenter's, by the way, is the spot where, according to local legend, the great author and surfcasting aficionado Jerry Sylvester suffered a fatal heart attack while fishing.

Just east of the bar is Deep Hole, where the bottom falls off green, and surf breaking over the left edge of the bar fades so quickly that any caster is reminded how easy it is to get into trouble. The hole is so large, so dramatic, that you are not going to miss it. Moreover, Carpenter's and Deep Hole are so close to one another, adjacent really, that most anglers rarely bother to distinguish between them. Deep Hole is a public fishing area with parking provided.

There is roughly a mile of beach between Deep Hole and the Matunuck West Wall. The eastern part of this is Matunuck State Beach, where there is ample parking. Access to that eastern section is from Succotash Road. The western portion, a stony, less inviting area for bathers, is a comfortable ramble on foot. All is legally accessible public property. The eastern border is the Harbor of Refuge guarded by a breakwater that reaches seaward for over ½ mile, which, season depending, is Matunuck's major contribution to local striper fishing.

Each spring, around the last week of April, the first school stripers make their appearance. These are the smallest, earliest migrants, and they come nowhere near keepable size with the regulations now in place. Schoolies as small as 12 inches, and rarely over 22, show up each season in astronomical numbers. I have seen dozens of surfmen lined up along the first 300 feet of jetty, facing west (the outside), each surf rod down hard with a thrashing schoolie. It is a traditional greeting place for first fish of the season and enjoys an uncommon reliability. The tradition of fishing there for stripers that small was established during a time when size limits were more liberal, when a keeper needed to be a mere 16 inches. Then, a large enough percentage of the fish that were caught were legal. But with the high fishing ethic that is observed today, I'm not sure if Matunuck's West Wall is any longer a viable fishing spot, as all fish at this time of year are throwbacks. I'm not sure it is good for the species to have so many people catching and releasing them with some mortality. This period of small fish is only a little over two weeks, followed quickly by larger bass and a few pre-spawning blues that will disappear quickly to some offshore spawning ground until summer. Look for fluke or summer flounder on the inside of the wall from July on. Years ago, when cod were available in greater numbers, I caught them there all winter with skimmer clams on the bottom, and March was the best month. But the cod have declined so dramatically that that is no longer possible.

CONTACT TIP: For information on Matunuck call Quaker Lane Sports, (800) 249-5400.

24
Harbor of Refuge
South Kingston, Rhode Island

BEST MONTHS TO FISH: May through November.
RECOMMENDED METHODS: Lures, live baits, and fly fishing.
FISH YOU CAN EXPECT TO CATCH: Stripers, bluefish, and fluke.
HOW TO GET THERE: For the west side, use Succotash Road from Route 1. For the east bank, take Route 1 to Route 108 south, then right on Galilee Road.

Salt Pond, as the Harbor of Refuge is sometimes called, is a major tidal estuary that reaches 5 miles inland. It is guarded by the West Wall (discussed in number 23) and the East Wall, at Point Judith; there is also a center wall with openings at each end that constrict water to produce substantial currents. Much of the harbor is shallow with only a small navigable channel for the sportfishing boats and the commercial fishing fleet that are moored there. These shallows, however, provide fertile opportunities for any number of forage species, which appeal to stripers throughout the season. For instance, there is an alewife run in spring; sea worms (nereis) are hatched out in June; and I have seen schools of bunker and tinker mackerel: Mars bars and Twinkies if you are a striped bass. While it is a famous spot for boat fishing in the deep of night when other traffic tends to be subdued, it can still be moderately productive for shore fishing.

Naturally, the greatest currents are at the narrowest places, which occur where the jetties meet the shore. It is possible to fish either bank, but the best access is on the east, or Galilee, side, near a restaurant called George's, which is famous for shore dinners. Here you'll find a short jetty where you can plug, jig, or drift bait in currents on either tide. I would not advise bottom fishing here because of currents that will push a sinker to shore too quickly. Just $\frac{1}{10}$ mile into the estuary from the docks that service the commercial fishing fleet, the widening of the channel and milder motion of the tide permit a bait and sinker to hold nicely. In this area, gurry is tossed over, or dispersed, from the fish houses, drawing baitfish and hungry stripers. For many years there has been a small group of hard-cores who quietly spirited out some huge linesides that would have made anybody's day. Of course, with the height of the dock above the water, it is necessary to have a long-handled gaff and very heavy lines—40-pound test or more—to keep such big fish from winding their way and your line among the crustaceans of the dock pilings. Squid is a popular bait here.

Along the swampy shore of the west side, it is possible to wade a couple of hundred feet toward the channel and lay a cast of chunk bait on the bottom, then free spool it to a sand spike and wait for Mr. Big to come along and eat it. A wise flycaster can wade these flats with a streamer, listening for the slurp of feeding bass. Both tides produce, but all my action on this Jerusalem side has been on the rise. The west side of the Harbor of Refuge is found at the far end of Matunuck's Succotash Road.

Back on the east side, if you take a right at the end of Galilee Road, you will come to the Great Island Bridge, which crosses a narrow opening that connects with a secondary tidal pond. Currents under this bridge are powerful, the area is well lighted, and the shadows underneath the bridge are a great spot for linesides to lie in ambush for baitfish. Once, during a night when I had gone to a number of places in search of stripers with no luck, I went there only to come upon the dark figure of a fish lurking in the shadow. Tossing my bucktail jig upstream in anticipation of where the current would take it, I watched it disappear in the maw of a decent fish of around 20 pounds. After a vicious tug of war, I beached it upcurrent. Then, fishing blind because I could no longer see any fish, I felt the take of four more stripers of comparable size! To this day, I can never fish the Harbor of Refuge or even drive through the town of Narragansett without keeping that spot honest.

For years there was an annual pollack run in late April when anglers gathered to take them in great numbers at sunset inside the harbor. If this species ever returns to the numbers of the past, this will be the spot to watch at this early time.

CONTACT TIP: For information on Matunuck call Quaker Lane Sports, (800) 249-5400.

25
Point Judith
Narragansett, Rhode Island

BEST MONTHS TO FISH: June through November.
RECOMMENDED METHODS: Plugs and lures, and some bait.
FISH YOU CAN EXPECT TO CATCH: Stripers, bluefish, porgy, and flounder.
HOW TO GET THERE: From Route 1, take Route 108 south to Point Judith, which is land's end.

One glance at the map will tell you that Point Judith juts prominently out into open water and that moving gamefish are likely to pass close to shore. This shallow stretch of rocky coast lies in the foreground of a Coast Guard station. With ample parking outside the gate, military authorities have never closed off access to the spot in the thirty-five years that I've known of it. One of those rare instances in which tradition has it that the best striper fishing is with popping plugs by day, low tide seems to have an edge by allowing casters to wade closer to a sea current that passes the lighthouse. To the right of the lighthouse foreground, facing open water, there is a drop-off, or hole, where the foam breaks over nearby bars, then fades with the newfound depth of the hole. It is a great place for a plug to be washed into—swimmers in the night, poppers during the day—as gamefish often gather there. A southeast wind would favor such a situation.

Some surfcasters also like to bait this hole with a chunk of menhaden or other traditional striper bait. Don't try this, however, if someone is plugging it or is already there with bait, as he or she is most likely having success with another choice of bait.

CAMP CRONIN

To the right of Point Judith, you'll see a breakwater that is sometimes called the East Wall; this is the other flanking jetty to the Harbor of Refuge (hot spot number 24). This undeveloped state park has spacious parking in full view of the jetty. The jetty is popular during the fall migration of stripers and bluefish. Both ends hold promise for deep night probing of the shoreline: the far end, because it has a current developed from the waters of the harbor, and at the shore, where the jetty meets land. It should be pointed out that the latter is often filled with a collection of weed that makes fishing impossible, but winds can change that. The East Wall is also a popular spot in summer for day fishing porgy and flounder.

CONTACT TIP: For information on this area call Quaker Lane Sports, (800) 249-5400.

26

Narragansett's Rocky Shore
Narragansett, Rhode Island

BEST MONTHS TO FISH: June through November.

RECOMMENDED METHODS: Lure casting.

FISH YOU CAN EXPECT TO CATCH: Stripers, bluefish, and occasional bonito.

HOW TO GET THERE: From Route 1, take Kingston Road or South Pier Road onto Ocean Road, Narragansett.

The rocky shore of Narragansett is a series of striper hot spots that begin at Point Judith and continue northeast into the mouth of Narragansett Bay. With the exception of Scarborough State Beach, there is little sand here until the town seawall, 5 miles up the coast at Narragansett Pier; still, the nooks and crannies of stone to the east of the state beach, beginning with Black Point, are popular spots. From then on, the ragged shoreline offers ample hiding places for forage species. Most stripers—fewer big fish during summer and larger numbers in autumn—are taken surprisingly close to the rocks. This brings us to a number of tactical considerations not yet covered in earlier pages.

Surfcasting along these rocky shorelines requires the angler to select a suitable landing spot before beginning to fish. Otherwise, the hooking of a large striper could turn out to be a disastrous experience. Most of the shore here is high enough above the water to make reaching down quite difficult, if not impossible. You'll need a long-handled gaff and a spot with lighter surf that's close enough to the water for gaffing. Otherwise, all successes will be confined to mediocre fish. But most noteworthy are the hazards unique to this kind of shoreline. It is very easy to trip on the rugged stones, and at the waterline, where black algae grows on the rocks, the footing is nearly always as slippery as ice. To make matters worse, once in the water, it is often impossible for a person to get out—and the sea will batter a person against the rocks, causing injuries that can easily lead to drowning. It is often observed here that your best bet in a moderate sea is to swim seaward in hope of being picked up. Thus, the conditions described above combine with the popularity of this area to make Narragansett the number-one killer of surfcasters on the Striper Coast, and this dubious distinction is earned over and over again, every season. Back to fishing.

Tradition dictates that fall is the best season here for stripers and blues, and daybreak the best time. Little attention is paid to the tide, and I know of no rule here that considers it. East and southeast winds—in the face—make fishing impossible. In October, commercial fish traps are put up with running lines set out from the Newton and Hazard Avenue shores. These lead migrating fish seaward, justifying the popular notion that few will be along the shore on the southwest sides of the net. As a result, people tend to fish on the left side of the net runners.

CONTACT TIP: Narragansett, Narrow River, and Harbor of Refuge questions can be answered by Quaker Lane Bait and Tackle, (401) 294-9642 or (800) 249-5400.

Live eels work at the mouth of Narrow River.

27
Narrow River Inlet
Narragansett, Rhode Island

BEST MONTHS TO FISH: June through November.

RECOMMENDED METHODS: Plugs, live eels, and fly fishing.

FISH YOU CAN EXPECT TO CATCH: Stripers, bluefish and hickory shad.

HOW TO GET THERE: Walk east, or left, along the sandy town beach from Narragansett.

Since we are still in Narragansett, it is necessary to distinguish between Narrow River and the rest of town, because there is so much to be said for this important section of seascape. This is, of course, another of those fertile estuaries that are loaded with the bait and foraging opportunities that our linesides so love.

When you look east from town—from what is known as Narragansett Pier, where the seawall ends and the town beach begins—the inlet is the last thing you see before the rocky shore starts up again. It can be approached by walking the beach from town or, if the guards at the gate of the exclusive Dunes Club are feeling charitable, by parking in the lot—after which you still have to walk east to the inlet. The southwest shore of the inlet is all sand, the opening guarded on this side by a series of bars before the bottom drops off to a deeper channel. In full view on the far bank, and slightly seaward, is a garage-sized stone called River Rock.

Local anglers like to take advantage of a dropping tide, fishing from the shallow bars and casting into the river's currents. Casts are made toward River Rock, then allowed to swing across the current to the eddy on the near side. Even with the tide way down, it is possible to free spool some line for a more distant drift.

As is so often the case, this is another one of those places where good fishing can be available on the incoming if linesides are lined up and panting on the outgoing. With currents sweeping around the point in the beach and hurrying to a rise on the inside, a beautiful rip forms where it is possible for a swimming plug to work itself into a frenzy; or you can drift an eel upriver. Timing for this alternate approach is high tide—anytime flood occurs in the evening, say, 7:00 to 10:00 in this location, and it will be a moon tide (new or full). Consequently, the amount of water exchanged will be maximized. This is all hold-your-rod fishing, a case of casting artificials as opposed to baiting and spiking a rod. This is also a great spot for fly fishing.

A couple of years ago, one early November night, I had some fresh pogies (menhaden) that I chunked and put on the bottom a couple of hundred yards short of the inlet so that sinkers wouldn't be swept by the tidal currents. Fishing with a pair of rods, hits from huge bluefish (14 to 16 pounds) were so fast and furious that I had to retire a rod and hold the one that remained.

An alternate approach to Narrow River Inlet is from the other bank—take the first right after Sprague Bridge when going north on Route 1A. While this is a public road, there are no-parking signs, and local residents—this does change with the seasons—usually call the police. There is also a small public lot at Sprague Bridge where it is possible to launch a canoe or kayak for the short paddle downstream. If you can get there, fishing from River Rock sometimes has an edge over the sandy side.

Every autumn, there is a run of hickory shad, and late winter brings a run of white perch that are caught in the headwaters a few miles upstream. Narrow River Inlet failed to earn a rating of four largely because of the difficulty of access, but it can sometimes provide some top-rate fishing.

CONTACT TIP: For information call Quaker Lane Sports, (800) 249-5400 or (401) 294-9642.

28

Beavertail (Conanicut Island)
Jamestown, Rhode Island

BEST MONTHS TO FISH: July through November.
RECOMMENDED METHODS: Plugs.
FISH YOU CAN EXPECT TO CATCH: Stripers, bluefish, blackfish (tautog), bonito, and albacore.

HOW TO GET THERE: Jamestown splits Narragansett Bay and is served by two bridges: The Jamestown Bridge spans the West Passage and the Newport Bridge the east. The town of Jamestown is immediately west of Newport Bridge and is your jump-off spot for the interstate from either direction. South into Jamestown, watch for signs pointing you to Beavertail, which is also to the south. From town go west on Narragansett Avenue then left to Southwest Avenue, turning right at its end to a place where there is water on both sides of the road (Mackerel Cove). Just follow your nose about three miles on Beavertail Road to the lighthouse.

On Jamestown, Beavertail Light is a classic striper spot with all the rocky shore hazards mentioned in the Narragansett section. This is a state park without parking fees, permits, or related governmental hassles. It is here that the old-time striper charters used to work the shore against a forbidding sea to cast swimming plugs toward the rocky shoreline. It is just as good from shore. Use swimming plugs at night for big bass; switch to poppers at early morning and during daylight. Fish right in front of the lighthouse, but don't hesitate to work the shoreline in either direction, especially if there's a touch of the mountain goat in your blood. Naturally, although this is a classic, well-known striper hot spot, expect bluefish as well as late-season bonito and albacore.

The entire south shore of Conanicut Island, from the tail east 5 miles to Fort Wetherill, is loaded with striper nooks and crannies. Both Hull and Mackerel coves are known for providing a continuation of the striper opportunity found at Beavertail. Some years, during the fall migration, bass will roam the sandy beach on the north edge of Mackerel Cove. Look for the cove on your left on the way out to the tail.

CONTACT TIP: For information call Quaker Lane Sports, (800) 249-5400 or (401) 294-9642.

29

Rome Point Outflow
North Kingston, Rhode Island

BEST MONTHS TO FISH FOR STRIPERS: June through October.

RECOMMENDED METHODS: Plugs and fly fishing.

FISH YOU CAN EXPECT TO CATCH: Stripers and blues.

HOW TO GET THERE: From Route 1A, go east on Waldron Avenue, taking a right at the end of the road. Drive south along the beach for about a half mile.

This is one of those places that people seem always to forget about; you will rarely see crowds fishing here. Best time is on the dropping tide that occurs during the night. What makes the falling waters really move here is the relative size of the outflow opening when compared to the size of the half mile estuary. Mid-tide the gut is barely 30 feet wide and the water flies past your waders once the tide ebbs.

Another consequence of the narrow inlet opening is that the lag in tide between what you will read on the tide chart and when the water turns is close to two hours. Anglers hoping to see the first dropping water don't need to be there until two hours after high water. The drive south along the beach, which is about a half mile, is not dry enough until then anyway because high tide floods a series of islands and shallow shoreline for most of the route south to the opening. A buggy or SUV is safer but a careful driver can make it down to the fishing with any auto.

Once the tide is about halfway down on the chart, it is possible to wade on the left or north side of the outflow, casting into the currents for gamefish waiting for a handout from the tide. Night tides it is best to use a floating Finnish swimmer for probing the spot. But don't waste your time fishing in the daytime. I also like to fly fish a streamer, casting across current and dead drifting under tension until my fly stops downstream. By the time you can wade, the water is shallow enough for the use of a much easier-to-use floating line.

CONTACT TIP: Call Quaker Lane Sports, (800) 249-5400 or (401) 294-9642.

30
Manchester Street Power Station
Providence River
Providence, Rhode Island

BEST MONTHS TO FISH FOR STRIPERS: December–March.

RECOMMENDED METHODS: Lure fishing. Stripers here like small Storm Shads in pearl and menhaden; also Cocahoe Minnows in glow and pearl patterns.

FISH YOU CAN EXPECT TO CATCH: School stripers, up to 25 pounds.

HOW TO GET THERE: Downtown Providence is in the midst of cross-bay construction and local highways, labeled in some way in relation to both Interstate 95 and 195, will probably figure into accessing these winter-over stripers. Access roads are under construction. Known as the hurricane barrier, people are really fishing the Manchester Street Power Station (look for the stacks). Watch for the Point Street Bridge and Al Forno Restaurant as key markers for this hot spot.

Providence River stripers can be taken all winter.

Because of the loss of traditional fishing at this time of year, winter-over, non-migratory fisheries are especially exciting. No one knows if the recent development of this fishery is a new phenomenon or is a new discovery of something that has always been there. But for about 15 years sharpies have been fishing for winter-over stripers south of the Point Street Bridge inside the hurricane barrier, north or on the city side of the barrier. Angling is carried out on both banks, and some of the jetty and bridge corners often hold collections of fish. It goes without saying that a set of unique hazards present themselves here. In the face of the night fishing imperative, angling in the seedy downtown of a big city carries its own set of dangers, which without suitable judgment border upon the hideous. Keep in mind that it is winter and night temperatures do no make for a fun-filled outing. Still, fishing is good during the day.

Regulars to the Providence River rely upon light- to medium-weight spinning tackle for the delivery of single-hook rubber shads. The rule is that the smaller the lure the better. Color preferences seem to be on the light side, perhaps because of the murky waters inherent to big-city fishing. These are inched slowly along the bottom. Most of the fish are schoolies but river leading fish caught there range to the upper 20-pound class. Regulations change over the years, but past history has been the statewide minimum size, with a two-striper limit. Presently, there are no season restrictions in this tidal river.

CONTACT TIP: Call the Providence store of Ocean State Tackle, (401) 272-2248.

31
Barrington River
Barrington, Rhode Island

BEST MONTHS TO FISH: May and June.
RECOMMENDED METHODS: Plugs and fly fishing.
FISH YOU CAN EXPECT TO CATCH: Stripers.
HOW TO GET THERE: From I–195 in East Providence, take Route 114 south into Barrington. The water on your left is the Barrington River. Watch for a crossover to access the northbound lane.

Emptying into the northeast corner of Narragansett Bay, the Barrington River illustrates the importance of estuarine rivers to the overall well-being of striped bass. During the lean spring season, when little forage is available along the coast, linesides tend to congregate in hot spots like this one to cash in on the feeding there. Grass shrimp, sperling, numerous species of mummichogs, and sea worms compose part of these forage opportunities, but the main draw is the many small stream runs of alewives that begin in April and expel spent fish until mid-June. Then, in fall, the young-of-the-season alewives are dropping down to touch off another feeding bonanza.

Needless to say, a striper hot spot is not made by feeding opportunities alone. With no industry or concentrated development along the immediate shore, eelgrass thrives, and water quality, when compared to similar parts of the coast, is surprisingly high. While some opportunity remains here throughout the bass season (May to November), the alewife runs are what make this river what it is. Schoolie fishing begins the first week in May and larger fish, 20 to 30 pounds, follow a few weeks later. Contrary to the popular belief that alewives are followed closely by stripers, it is the spent fish—the easy ones to catch—that the bigger linesides are looking to cash in on, and these are not available until late May or early June.

The Barrington tends to get more fishing pressure than its counterpart, the Warren, because of accessibility, what with roads along most shorelines. The Massasoit Avenue Bridge, near the white church off Route 114, is sometimes used. Upriver (north of the church), One Hundred Acre Cove, a grassy marsh in plain view from Route 114, harbors good numbers of small fish in some early seasons. Just above Barrington, from the northbound lane of the Wampanoag Trail, you will see a nature walk that leads to a point that guards the more open parts of One Hundred Acre Cove. There is a nice tide rip here on the mid-incoming for light tackle, particularly for fly fishing. South on Route 114 about 2 miles, behind the Barrington police station, it is possible to drift bait in the river from an old railroad bridge that is now used as a bike path. In early June, the regulars there can be seen in the deep night nodding over rods that trail sea worms in the current.

CONTACT TIP: Call the Providence store of Ocean State Tackle, (401) 272-2248.

32
Warren River
Warren, Rhode Island

BEST MONTHS TO FISH: May and June.
RECOMMENDED METHODS: Alewife simulators, sea worms, plugs, and fly fishing.
FISH YOU CAN EXPECT TO CATCH: Stripers and white perch.
HOW TO GET THERE: From I–195 in East Providence, take Route 114 south into Barrington. The second river bridge that you drive over spans the Warren River, which serves as the town line separating Barrington and Warren.

Because the Warren and Barrington rivers are fork rivers that join, their estuarine nature, bait potential, and fishing opportunities are remarkably similar. Like the Barrington, the Warren has good bridge fishing from the same bike path that used to be a railroad bridge. The Route 114 bridge for both rivers is utilized on the outgoing tide; there is also good schoolie fishing farther upstream.

The Warren enjoys a slightly greater amount of tidal exchange but less access opportunity than the Barrington. With regard to fishing from the bridges, the bike-path bridge has a slight edge and must be fished during the incoming tide. This is a short bridge, and it is a simple matter to walk a good catch to shore on either end for landing. Baits used are usually sea worms. Time was when alewives were popular but that has been outlawed to preserve the runs. Now the fishing is mostly sea worms in the current, adding the correct amount of split shot to drift at the right level for stripers.

Naturally, if the incoming water holds fish, you can usually expect the outgoing to yield. However, the Route 114 bridge—for falling-tide fishing—presents tougher landing opportunities, and you'll have to do some fancy climbing down to the water if the bass you've got is a big one.

Few anglers know that the marshy shore north of the Warren River bike-path bridge can be highly productive casting from the east bank. During a falling tide, it is possible to throw an alewife simulating rubber shad upcurrent, permitting a drift until it is fully downtide, where big fish will pick it up and move off. A caster with a popping plug at dawn will bring up small fish on either tide, and I can think of no better spot for fly casting than the shallows on the east bank of the river above the trestle. Fly fishing works either tide, but a falling tide can mean big trouble if the lineside is a good one and you hook up too close to the bridge. If it were not for the smell of salt, you might imagine yourself on a river in Europe. At the right times, the river could be rated four, but this hot spot had to be penalized due to its short season. The best fish here, though not all that common, weigh in around the low forties, and one's chances for that kind of fish improve downriver.

Of less importance is a sizable white perch run in March; the perch can be taken way upriver in Seekonk, on the small back road bridge just below I–195. Fish the bottom with a sea-worm bit.

CONTACT TIP: Call the Bristol store of Ocean State Tackle, (401) 254-6066.

33

Colt Drive State Park
Bristol, Rhode Island

BEST MONTHS TO FISH FOR STRIPERS: May through July.
RECOMMENDED METHODS: Plugs, live eels and fly fishing.
FISH YOU CAN EXPECT TO CATCH: Stripers and blues.
HOW TO GET THERE: From Route 114 in Bristol, turn west into Colt State Park at a gate with two life-sized bronze bull statues at the entrance.

As a highly accessible public shore road on the east bank of Narragansett Bay, Colt Drive leads to a set of two bridges spanning an outflow from a clean salt pond that fills on the rising tide. This estuary is loaded with grass shrimp, sperling and indigenous crustaceans. Season and opportunity depending, juvenile crabs, worm hatches, peanut bunker, and late-summer snapper blues will camp in the back pond, drawing stripers and bluefish into outflow currents. Known years ago as Mill Gut, we have fished this location off and on for 50 years. But we had to drop this spot from the first edition of *Striper Hot Spots* when Rhode Island DEM closed the park to access during the night hours when there was the best fishing. More recently, the state has built a public boat-launching ramp at the north end of the park, which had customary night use, and they were forced to reopen the park after hours for fishing.

As with so many outflows, the best fishing is on the falling tide. Regulars will drift live eels off of the bayside bridge out to a mussel bar. You can see the bar appearing as a ruffle of water about 100 yards west. Once the water has dropped a little, it is possible to wade out to this bar and cast swimming plugs or flies across the current. Bass often gather downcurrent of the bar to face the flow and feed upon whatever is in the marine smorgasbord. Some nights the bass will follow the current upstream into the pond, and near the end of the tide they will be dropping down. You can hear them slurping. Late May and June, some years, there is a worm hatch in the pond that creates a piscatorial pandemonium but I dislike these juvenile worms all over the seascape by the thousands because all it does is concentrate a lot of stripers amid a billion little worms that are difficult to compete with. It is the kind of fishing, the kind of frustration, that has you telling your friends you were not there. But if you are to simulate a worm, only the fly rod can deliver what is needed. Waters are shallow here so a floating fly line is fine.

CONTACT TIP: Call the Bristol store of Ocean State Tackle, (401) 254-6066.

34

Bristol Narrows
Bristol, Rhode Island

BEST MONTHS TO FISH: May through October.

RECOMMENDED METHODS: Sea worms, chunks, swimming plugs, and fly fishing.

FISH YOU CAN EXPECT TO CATCH: Blackfish (tautog), stripers, and bluefish.

HOW TO GET THERE: Bristol Narrows is south of Warren. Take a left turn onto Narrows Road off Route 136 southbound.

Bristol Narrows is another "secret spot" for tautog few Rhody anglers know.

Access to the Narrows, which is really the west bank of the mouth of the Kickemuit River, is by way of a sandbar that is exposed at low tide. People like to drive onto the bar either to launch their boats or to fish from shore. It is not soft or dangerous, but failure to move that vehicle when the tide begins coming back could spoil your day.

In late April, there is a blackfish spawning run that is Rhode Island's worst-kept secret. Shoulder to shoulder with fifty other fishermen, it is possible to fill a bucket with tautog ranging from 3 to 12 pounds. An absolute requirement is that you fish the outgoing tide with sea worms and never cast more than 30 feet. This is group sport where mutual cooperation is mandatory. Fish with a thick skin and be polite or the others will use you for bait—and they prefer chunks.

Other than an occasional couple of romantic kids, there is little activity at night here, but often the linesides of Mount Hope Bay will forage in the shallows or lurk in the currents that form from the Kickemuit River. Except for the aforementioned tautog fishing, which is all done during the day, any tide in which water is moving in the deep night when things are quiet has potential. A steady producer in spring through June is a bunker chunk on a 7/0 hook (mono leader) drifted in the currents. Let any fish that picks it up move off 10 yards before whacking it. You can also do well with swimming plugs. In either case, because this river has an alewife run of its own that lures big bass up from Mount Hope Bay, be ready for some moby linesides at times or you will cry. Because of the alewife run, spring has an edge, but I have still seen good stripers here all summer in lesser numbers. As is so much the case elsewhere, blues often take up slack left by stripers.

This is another great fly-rod spot because of its good wading, natural protection (to allay surf), and attractive currents. No hassles. Remember that if this were a tautog book, Bristol Narrows would be rated five.

CONTACT TIP: Call the Bristol store of Ocean State Tackle, (401) 254-6066.

35

Brenton Point State Park
Newport, Rhode Island

BEST MONTHS TO FISH: From July on, but especially October and November.

RECOMMENDED METHODS: Plugs, green crabs, or seaworms.

FISH YOU CAN EXPECT TO CATCH: Stripers, bluefish, and blackfish.

HOW TO GET THERE: From 138 in Newport, take Route 238 (Thames Street) south for two miles until the name changes to Carroll

Avenue and continue until Ocean Avenue where you take a right. Travel west for 1½ miles to Brenton Point.

This area offers ½ mile of rocky shore that is excellent habitat for stripers and bluefish. While the coastal structure is similar to Narragansett's, the water here is more shallow, and perhaps less dangerous—but still good cover for stripers and baitfish in the nook-and-cranny shoreline. Regulars prefer eels, both live and rigged, along with swimming plugs. Day anglers—and their prospects get better as the season progresses—use poppers. Surfcasters who know how to read water can excel here. A hot item at this writing is the Mambo Minnow in the largest size. No particular tide favors this spot, but any moderate onshore wind—southeast to west—helps. Look for good blackfish opportunities with green crabs as bait in late October.

CONTACT TIP: Saltwater Edge, (401) 842-0062, is a great fly shop here that knows the ropes and takes fly fishers on guided trips.

36
Fort Adams State Park
Newport, Rhode Island

BEST MONTHS TO FISH: From July on, but especially October and November.

RECOMMENDED METHODS: Plugs.

FISH YOU CAN EXPECT TO CATCH: Stripers and bluefish.

HOW TO GET THERE: From 138 in Newport, take Route 238 (Thames Street) south for two miles, then take a right or west onto Harrison Avenue. Follow the signs to Fort Adams State Park.

Fort Adams is more protected, more into the bay, than Brenton Point. The flatter and shallower water that results from this often demands the cover of darkness for feeding stripers to use it. But, under the cover of darkness, there are feeding stripers and blues along the west edge of the park, which is the shore of Narragansett Bay's east passage. Entrance is sometimes limited at night, but officials generally do not deny access to people equipped for fishing at any hour. This spot is a good alternative if a nasty east wind should kick up, spoiling the fishing at Brenton Point. Also, menhaden, which frequent Narragansett Bay, will sometimes give this spot an edge. It is a good idea to combo up the fort with Brenton and watch them both, as they are just far enough apart to provide similar though unique opportunities.

CONTACT TIP: Anglers using traditional methods can contact Beachfront Bait and Tackle, (401) 849-4665.

BLOCK ISLAND

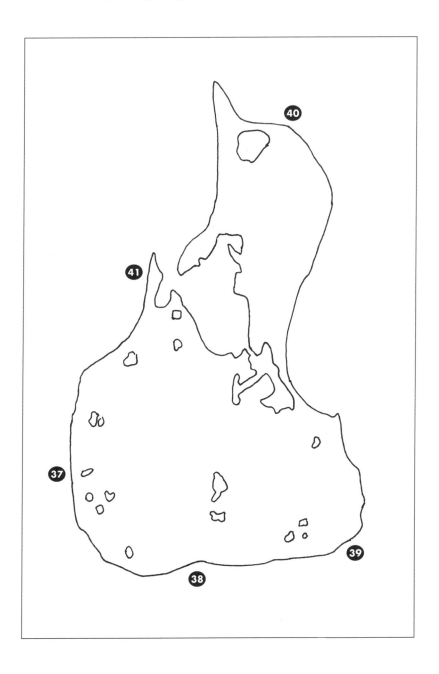

Block Island

Just 17 miles east of Montauk and 12 miles south of Rhode Island, Block Island has only recently come into its own as an attractive, or at least well-known, surfcasting spot. During the late seventies and early eighties, when striper opportunities were drying up everywhere else, the "Block" provided some memorable encounters with moby stripers. Indeed, it was probably the twilight of striper fishing's glory days.

I've had to make some painful decisions regarding exactly which spots to include here. In spite of overt efforts by some to protect a number of locations where shore fishing takes place regularly, I just had too many places. Safety was the reason for dropping Sandy Point; in the case of Mohegan Bluffs, I combined several related spots. Indeed, that whole south shore is so replete with points and coves as to render the area, much to my delight, one great hot spot.

The island is not a be-all and end-all location, because logistics raise the price of going there well beyond what some are willing to pay. There is only one ferry that carries autos in fall, and if the weather turns bad, that vessel may not run. Dyed-in-the-wool island fishermen like to keep one junker for their "inner circle" to use in the fall. (I wonder what Rhode Island's new mandatory insurance law will do to that tradition.) Others leave the family auto behind and one member loses transportation for a few weeks while the other takes daily flights out of Westerly. No doubt a string of consecutive storms, ending the season by sheer default of time, will send an angler on a retrieval trip that lacks the luster of having some fishing thrown in, what with Christmas so close. Renting a place for the season, the gang all tosses money into the pot; this is the least of all expenses.

There are fewer fish but more charm in summer, when the weather is safer. Ferries operate out of Newport and New London on a seasonal basis. The only year-round ferry, the one that keeps this place alive, comes daily from Galilee, Rhode Island, and it carries cars.

37
Southwest Point
Block Island, Rhode Island

BEST MONTHS TO FISH: June through November.
RECOMMENDED METHODS: Plugs.
FISH YOU CAN EXPECT TO CATCH: Stripers.
HOW TO GET THERE: From Old Harbor, take Ocean Avenue, then left onto Beach Avenue to a left onto Center Road. Take a right onto Cooneymus Road and follow it to land's end. There are any number of undeveloped trails that will lead to Southwest Point. All are complicated and some are even embroiled in legal controversy, but any left at the end of Cooneymus will lead to suitable parking. Walk the shore south, or left, until opposite a red bell buoy about 400 feet from shore. This marks Southwest Point.

Southwest Point is thought to be a very good spot on the island because it can provide opportunities for bigger stripers; however, this rocky shore can accommodate so few anglers that I am forced to rate it somewhat lower than I might otherwise. Past performance has given it a reputation for big bass that it can't always live up to. A maddening aspect of this spot, as with any productive spot of similar size, is that crowds have a way of ruining the fishing. Dropping tides are popular with southwest winds. Increase the rating by one or two for November fishing.

CONTACT TIP: Call Twin Maples, (401) 466-5547, for an island overview.

38
Mohegan Bluffs
Block Island, Rhode Island

BEST MONTHS TO FISH: June through November.

RECOMMENDED METHODS: Plugs.

FISH YOU CAN EXPECT TO CATCH: Stripers and bluefish.

HOW TO GET THERE: From Old Harbor, take Ocean Avenue, then left onto Beach Avenue to a left onto Center Road. After the airport, the road becomes Lakeside Drive, which you follow south for another mile to its end for a right onto Black Rock Road. You'll know the right turn because of the 3-foot painted stone at the intersection. Park where you can, at places where there is the greatest evidence of use. The road is close to the bluff at Black Rock.

This spot is really an area comprising three well-known hot spots: Black Rock, Spar Point, and Snake Hole. All provide a similar alternating rock-and-sand structure at the base of the south shore Mohegan Bluffs. Because there is so much here, the seasoned surfcaster can read for suitable striper-holding water and fish only what he or she likes. Like the roads leading here, none of these places has signs announcing its identity; once you've climbed down the cliffs, it is hard to locate suitable landmarks if you're not familiar with the rocky shoreline. While the fishing here is not quite as good as at Southwest Point, the area compensates with its ability to accommodate any number of anglers, which means plenty of room to fish in peace. Look for the blues to arrive in mid-July and improve with the season.

CONTACT TIP: Call Twin Maples, (401) 466-5547.

39
Southeast Light
Block Island, Rhode Island

BEST MONTHS TO FISH: August through November.
RECOMMENDED METHODS: Popping plugs.
FISH YOU CAN EXPECT TO CATCH: Bluefish and occasional stripers.
HOW TO GET THERE: From Old Harbor, go south on Southeast Road until you reach public parking near the lighthouse.

This is a tough spot to climb down into, but when blues couldn't be found anywhere else in the late sixties, I was catching them here in daylight with poppers. The rocky shore is loaded with highly readable water that also holds stripers, but don't expect them until after dark. I suggest you become familiar with the shore by daylight in one of those rare spots where you can have day fishing; then try the stripers once you've learned your way around. They say that a 60-plus lineside was taken here in the early-eighties heyday of island fall fishing. But there is so much protectionism and fairy lore here that few local anglers are willing to talk about anything, so I doubt we'll ever know. My first Block Island striper—an 18-pounder in 1969—came from between Mohegan Bluffs and the lighthouse, an area sometimes called Corn Cove.

CONTACT TIP: Call Twin Maples, (401) 466-5547.

40
Grove Point
Block Island, Rhode Island

BEST MONTHS TO FISH: June through November.
RECOMMENDED METHODS: Plugs.
FISH YOU CAN EXPECT TO CATCH: Stripers and occasional bluefish.
HOW TO GET THERE: From Old Harbor, take Corn Neck Road north for nearly 4 miles. Once Sachem Pond is visible on your left, you'll see state land on the ocean side to your right just before the paved portion of the road ends.

You'll have to use a cast-and-walk system of feeling the place out, but the entire rocky shoreline in this area can hold stripers at times. I'm convinced that much of what was learned by surfcasters here was taught to them by boat fishermen who were just a little farther off shore. My old striper buddy Ray Jobin, as competent a striperman as I've ever known, did a job there regularly in the late sixties. If you can locate a mussel bar, the early incoming tide can be productive. Avoid an east wind unless it is light and in an early stage of development.

CONTACT TIP: Call Twin Maples, (401) 466-5547.

41
Inlet to Great Salt Pond (the Cut)
Block Island, Rhode Island

BEST MONTHS TO FISH: June through November.
RECOMMENDED METHODS: Fly fishing, light spinning, and bait.
FISH YOU CAN EXPECT TO CATCH: Stripers, blues, bonito, little tunny, and fluke.
HOW TO GET THERE: Go west on Ocean Avenue, take a left onto Side Road for ½ mile, then go right on Champlins Road all the way out to the Coast Guard station. Park at the last corner.

The Coast Guard Channel of the salt pond into New Harbor, a close walking distance, is considered the best shore fishing spot on the island. The Cut, as it is fondly known, is most popular with fly anglers and pluggers who fish from the jetty to the Coast Guard Station. Best tides are reputed to be moving water, mid-tide, going either way. Though the target species remains stripers, fishing for bonito, and some years little tunny—two highly selective species—

can be quite reliable. Small lures and flies seem to work best. Epoxy patterns are very popular in Great Salt Pond once the bonito appear. The jetty there is not suitable for fishing because of height from the water, condition of rocks, and the slime. Even if you hooked a good fish, you would never get it in.

Located south of the entrance to New Harbor's salt pond, the ½-mile sandy stretch of shore known as Charlestown Beach provides some good chunk fishing for bass at night and fluke fishing with chubs and squid strips during the day.

CONTACT TIP: Call Twin Maples, (401) 466-5547.

MARTHA'S VINEYARD

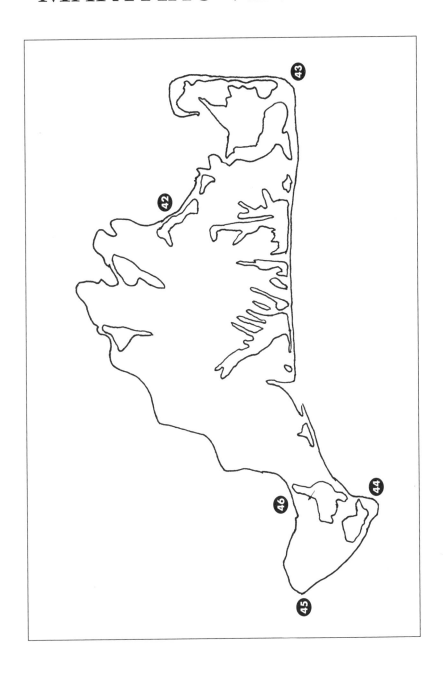

Martha's Vineyard

Of the offshore islands of consequence, each can lay claim to a certain unique quality: Block Island is largely undiscovered; Nantucket is the most charming; the Vineyard celebrates surfcasting with terrific enthusiasm. Very soon after leaving the ferry, it becomes excitingly evident to any shore fisherman that surfcasting is alive and well on Martha's Vineyard. Pat Abate, an old-guard Cape surfcasting comrade from another life, says, "It's the only place I have ever gone where they cheer and embrace fishermen as though they were a high school team."

Part of the Vineyard that didn't make the cut was the entire south shore because so much of it is private property. I would like to have included a treatment of the great pond openings in spring, when the past year's alewives are panting to get out and the present season's are straining to make it in—stripers cutting through the emerald walls of sea while sweet water mingles. Another hard choice was Cape Poge, which had to be left out because of limited parking and difficult access, especially during the piping plover mating season.

I am, of course, indebted to the late Robert Post, the author of an unforgettably charming collection of Vineyard surf-fishing portraits in his book *Reading the Water*. When reading Dr. Post, one develops an appreciation for both natural history and the island's rich lore. Indeed, he engages his reader on any number of levels while never losing touch with a simple, folksy style that irrevocably touches something in each of us. Yet the mission of worshipping at the altar of surfcasting is never more than a cast away. Thus, while you wend your way along the streets and shores of the Vineyard, you are unwittingly taking the medicine of enlightenment while tasting the sweetness of play. It is a Dr. Post skill that I feel privileged to share with you here because he wrote the Vineyard spots.

42
Vineyard Bridges
Oak Bluffs and Edgartown
Martha's Vineyard, Massachusetts

BEST MONTHS TO FISH: May, June, September, and October.

RECOMMENDED METHODS: Fly fishing, eels, jigs, small plugs, needlefish, Hopkins, and Kastmasters.

FISH YOU CAN EXPECT TO CATCH: Stripers, bluefish, bonito, and false albacore.

HOW TO GET THERE: Little Bridge, Joseph Sylvia State Beach, and Anthiers Bridge (also known as Big Bridge) are located on the northeast side of the island. Access and parking are available year-round parallel to the beach for 1½ miles. Take New York Avenue to Seaview Avenue, which becomes Beach Road. Little Bridge is located at the Oak Bluffs end of Beach Road, and Anthiers Bridge is at the Edgartown end. State Beach is between them.

Because this area faces Nantucket Sound, high surf is rare. Beach Road is really a paved-over barrier beach between the sound and Sengekontacket Pond, one of the primary sources of bay scallops on the Vineyard.

The inlets and jetties that serve the pond's water are located at each bridge, where baitfish are usually running in and out with the tides. What makes this stretch of beach unique is the variety of methods anglers can try here in their quest for hooking gamefish.

Bridge fishing is popular on Anthiers. One technique is to drift eels over the side by letting them run with the tide; this is especially effective with stripers and blues in the fall. Fish with an open bail, applying finger pressure to the line so that you can allow a short run before setting the hook. Then, carefully work yourself off the bridge so you can better fight and land a fish from the beach.

In the 1960s, the late author and inventor Al Reinfelder developed an effective technique for fishing his Bait Tail jigs from bridges. Favoring the uptide side of the bridge that faced the oncoming water, Al's technique required heavy tackle, what with the fish having the tendency to go with the current under the bridge and around the pilings. Al once wrote, "Fish take feeding positions on both sides of the bridge, but rarely in the middle, directly beneath the span. Since fish always face the current, those on the front of the bridge face away from the bridge, while those on the back face the bridge directly" (*Bait Tail Fishing*, 1969). This doesn't mean one won't get the attention of a striper on the "back side" of a bridge, but the chance of fighting and landing a fish successfully increases if one doesn't have to fight pilings and other bridge obstructions.

In early spring, some of the first schoolie stripers of the season arrive at Anthiers Bridge Inlet to Sengekontacket Pond. Fly-rod fishermen have success off the jetties and on the beach fronting the pond. Sand eel and 1-inch orange worm imitations (it is worm spawn-out time) work best. Spin fishermen should stick to light tackle with jigs or small swimmers. Late-summer and fall fishing improves with the arrival of the daylight feeders—bonito and false albacore. These unpredictable gamesters can hit at any tide, but early morning outgoing or high slack seem to produce best. Flies, Swedish Pimples, and needlefish should produce a hookup.

The 1½-mile stretch of sandy beach between the bridges is also a fine area for bottom fishing with cut bait. Pick a pleasant fall night and bring a beach chair and a cooler with food and drink. After several minutes—or several hours—you may hook up with a monster bluefish or giant cow bass. Sometimes it pays to be innovative if the fish aren't hitting. Many years ago, a fisherman who had run through all his bait was left with nothing but a foil-wrapped cigar. After putting a hook through it, he dropped it over the side of Anthiers Bridge and caught a fine striped bass.

CONTACT TIP: Larry's Tackle Shop, (508) 627-5088, is a Vineyard fly-fishing headquarters.

Dick's Bait and Tackle, (508) 693-7669, in Oak Bluffs can also report on Vineyard surf fishing.

43
Wasque Point
Edgartown, Martha's Vineyard, Massachusetts

BEST MONTHS TO FISH: May through November.

RECOMMENDED METHODS: Joppa Jigs, swimming plugs, eels, tins, and popping plugs.

FISH YOU CAN EXPECT TO CATCH: Stripers and bluefish.

HOW TO GET THERE: If using a buggy, take a right off Main Street in Edgartown onto Katama Road and follow it to land's end at South Beach. There, on the left, you'll find a marked beach path for vehicles. Those without a beach vehicle can take a left onto North Water Street, then a left onto Daggett for the Chappy Ferry. Once across, take Chappaquiddick Road for 2½ miles to a right onto Poucha Road and then a left onto Wasque Road (dirt road), where there is a Trustees of Reservation booth marking the entrance to Wasque. Anglers with their gear can walk the ²⁄₁₀ mile to the sandy beach along a marked path.

Open water and Nantucket Sound collide at Wasque, forming a tremendous rip. The last four hours of a falling tide (east to west) are the most popular. Regulars particularly like this tide when it combines with a strong southwest wind, which causes the rip to kick up, making bait more vulnerable and seemingly causing gamefish to attack more reliably.

Because of the crowds that collect there when stripers and blues are running, artificials are the only method that can be used. (Some will fish bait briefly among light crowds at slack tide.) Occasional stripers are taken during the day, but Wasque's better fish usually hit at night. In spring, it is a case of watching for bait arrivals—herring, then squid. By then, there should be a good striper population surging through the rips. Joppa Jigs, which are produced locally, work magic during the first arrivals. Then Gibbs Swimmers, Atoms, and Dannys dominate, as the linesides get bigger with the progressing season.

Bluefish, it seems, hold up all summer, providing fairly consistent action even during the day. Hopkins, Kastmasters, Ballistic Missiles, Roberts Casting Plugs, and Atom poppers—all chosen to produce casting distance—will bring them up. Hooked fish take advantage of the current running strong to the right. Let downtide surfcasters know that you are on and that you are coming down so that you can safely follow and keep the fish in front of you. They should be willing to reel in line and yield.

While the fishing is predominantly blues and stripers (in that order), bonito and false albacore are sometimes taken during August and September, but these are uncommon showings. Similarly, on October 30, 1986, Dan Colli hooked and landed a 68-pound yellowfin tuna on a Spofford Ballistic Missile while casting for bluefish. In the late 1960s, islander Dick Hathaway almost landed a giant sturgeon, estimated to weigh around 200 pounds.

To use a buggy, both a Dukes County beach sticker and a Wasque Point Trustees of Reservation Oversand Vehicle Permit are required. Obey all regulations because rare or endangered piping plovers or least terns may be nesting. As a result, this spot is definitely subject to intermittent closings as various branches of government and private interests grapple with management of endangered bird species. It may be necessary to check on the status of Wasque through tackle shops or the Chamber of Commerce.

CONTACT TIP: Dick's Bait and Tackle, (508) 693-7669, in Oak Bluffs can report on Vineyard surf fishing.

44
Squibnocket Point
Chilmark, Martha's Vineyard, Massachusetts

BEST MONTHS TO FISH: May through mid-June, and mid-September through mid-November.

RECOMMENDED METHODS: Large swimming plugs and eels.

FISH YOU CAN EXPECT TO CATCH: Stripers and bluefish.

HOW TO GET THERE: Head southwest on State Road to South Road in Chilmark. Two miles past Beetlebung Corner, take a left onto Squibnocket Road (marked by a granite pillar). This road ends at the town parking lot on Squibnocket Bight. The lot is restricted to town residents during the summer tourist season.

To the right of the parking lot is a 2-mile stretch of excellent striper fishing. Start by casting in "The Bowl"—to the right of the parking area—on the incoming tide at dusk, then work your way down to the "Mussel Bed." This is the same area described by Jerry Jansen, surf-fishing pioneer and author of *Successful Surf Fishing*, published in 1934.

Baitfish are almost always present in "The Bowl," and in the fall this spot is absolutely thick with bait. Extending around The Bowl is a rock and sand bar covered with mussel beds. This bar is a highly favored spot, and it can be waded from dead low tide until the rising water gets too rough. Don't try this unless you are in the company of someone who has been out there a few times. The best tide here is the rising and as much of it as you can stand. No matter what the tide, however, get there before sunup and stick it out until daylight. If the fish are going to hit, they will do so before light and will quit right after it gets light enough to see. The Mussel Bed is a prime spot for night fishing. All the beach up to Squibnocket Point is excellent, being full of the rocks and holes so dearly loved by bass and surf anglers. Around the point, the "beach" is a sloping wall of round rocks with a few sandy spots here and there. It is an excellent place to fish, but you may run into private property.

Remember that the Massachusetts Colonial Ordinance (1641–47) gave anglers the right of trespass. "The public may also pass over privately owned land below the mean high-tide mark for the purpose of fishing, fowling, and navigation. The courts have ruled, however, that walking the beach and bathing are not among the public rights in the intertidal zone" (source: "Public Access to the Waters of Massachusetts," Department of Fisheries, Wildlife, and Environmental Law Enforcement, page 2). Nevertheless, I avoid using this spot during the bathing season.

In the late 1800s, Squibnocket Point was the location of two prestigious bass clubs: the Squibnocket Club, with eight bass stands, and the Providence Club, with three. These provided a gathering place to fish and socialize in the period following the Civil War. "Stands for the most part were made by driving steel rods into the rocks to support narrow wooden walkways. At the end of each walkway was a small platform from which the angler cast" (from *The Complete Book of Striped Bass Fishing,* Hal Lyman and Frank Woolner). A chummer and a gaffer assisted the angler. The clubs died out around 1897, when striped bass went into one of their notorious periods of population decline and almost vanished from the New England coast.

Although plugging at night will usually produce only striped bass and an occasional bluefish, in 1983 Vineyard fisherman Whit Manter hooked up to a shark on a Danny plug. After a heart-pounding, knee-knocking battle, the 212-pound, 7-foot 9-inch monster was landed.

CONTACT TIP: Larry's Tackle Shop, (508) 627-5088, is a Vineyard fly-fishing headquarters.

Dick's Bait and Tackle, (508) 693-7669, in Oak Bluffs can also report on Vineyard surf fishing.

45
Gay Head Cliffs/Pilots Landing
Gay Head, Martha's Vineyard, Massachusetts

BEST MONTHS TO FISH: June, July, October, and November.

RECOMMENDED METHODS: Poppers, swimming plugs, eels, and large black needlefish.

FISH YOU CAN EXPECT TO CATCH: Stripers and bluefish.

HOW TO GET THERE: Located on the southwest-facing side of the Vineyard, this area is reached by taking State Road to South Road, which ends in a loop. At the bottom of the loop, across from public restrooms, there is town parking that anglers can use evenings. To the right of the parking lot is the beach access boardwalk, which is owned by the Martha's Vineyard Land Bank, and which you have to stay on.

Surfcasting is celebrated on Martha's Vineyard.

Once on the beach, walk ½ mile to the right to Southwest Rock. At this point, on a coming tide, the Atlantic sweeps into Vineyard Sound, creating a small rip off the point. If you keep walking right, you'll find the next ½ mile to be prime fishing. Fish the rock piles, the bowl, and the next point, which is Pilots Landing. Gay Head Cliffs and Pilots Landing are dusk-to-dawn hot spots. Change of light may produce on any tide, but top of the tide—last two hours of incoming—will produce best through the night. Checking the type of bait in the water could help you with lure selection. Nights when mullet have been visible, large swimming plugs have produced. If sand eels are abundant, try a needlefish plug, an eel, or a teaser fly tied off a barrel swivel in front of a swimming plug.

The cliffs here are a national treasure and landmark. Rising 150 feet from sea level, they are the highest cliffs on the Atlantic Coast, and a lighthouse stands guard at the peak. The varied colors of the clay that slopes down to the beach make for a spectacular fishing spot. Once part of the Algonquin nation, these cliffs are now within the Gay Head Wampanoag Indian Lands. The fragile cliffs are considered sacred ground by the Indians, so do not attempt to walk down them. Also, it is dangerous and contributes to erosion.

In the 1950s, it was not uncommon to catch codfish and pollack from the surf here. Vineyard fisherman Kib Bramhall recalls pollack being so abundant that a Pollack Derby ran the week after the Striped Bass and Bluefish Derby ended. Bramhall says, "It centered around Menemsha and Gay Head and was run by Manuel Lima, who was an ardent islander fisherman." From the late 1970s until 1984, weakfish made a return and were abundant, enabling anglers to catch stripers, blues, and weaks in a single trip.

CONTACT TIP: Larry's Tackle Shop, (508) 627-5088, is a Vineyard fly-fishing headquarters.

Dick's Bait and Tackle, (508) 693-7669, in Oak Bluffs can also report on Vineyard surf fishing.

46
Lobsterville Beach and Jetty
Gay Head, Martha's Vineyard, Massachusetts

BEST MONTHS TO FISH: June through October.
RECOMMENDED METHODS: Joppa Jigs, small swimming plugs, Swedish Pimples, eels, fresh bait, and fly fishing.

FISH YOU CAN EXPECT TO CATCH: Stripers, bluefish, bonito, and false albacore.

HOW TO GET THERE: Lobsterville Beach is located on the northwest side (but to the southwest) fronting Vineyard South and Menemsha Bight. Take State Road to South Road, then right onto Lobsterville Road. Go ¾ mile to "Bend-in-the-Road," which is a public parking area for Town Beach. To reach the jetty at Menemsha Pond, continue along Lobsterville Road and bear left onto West Basin Road. There are marked parking spaces near the jetty. Be sure to observe the no-parking signs along these roads.

From the Town Beach parking area, anglers can walk ¾ mile to the left until they reach Dogfish Bar, or they can walk 1½ miles to the right to the jetties. The entire beach will produce, but the fishing will improve as concentrations of bait increase. Calm water and an abundance of baitfish moving in and out of Menemsha Pond have made this area one of the premier fly-fishing spots on the East Coast. White and yellow Lefty's Deceivers work best.

Spring is best for school stripers. Later in the season, locals like a falling tide after dark. In August, big bass often go up into the pond across from the Coast Guard station. There are good results here at night casting eels, or, if you can snag some bunker (pogie), drift them live in the channel. Stay in free spool or open bail with a finger controlling the line, and when you feel it move off from a take, count to ten and give it a whack. I often use a double-hook setup for blues, which, when they go into a frenzy, will often share the pogie so that you can catch two at once. With blues, use wire leaders of 50- or 80-pound test. For stripers, 50-pound mono leaders are preferred.

While the blues hit best at dawn and dusk, bonito and false albacore feed during the day at the jetty from late July until mid-October. Because they are unpredictable and finicky feeders, plan on spending many hours seeking a hookup. But we've found that fresh bait—such as tinker mackerel and sand eels—on a number 8 or 10 treble hook works well. Of artificials, the most successful are the Spofford Needlefish with a slow retrieve and the Swedish Pimple with a very rapid one.

Calm nights on the pond, when the water is clear, check for bait. Instead of sand eels, you may be rewarded with the rare sighting of a baby lobster migration on the ocean floor.

CONTACT TIP: Larry's Tackle Shop, (508) 627-5088, is a Vineyard fly-fishing headquarters.

Dick's Bait and Tackle, (508) 693-7669, in Oak Bluffs can also report on Vineyard surf fishing.

NANTUCKET

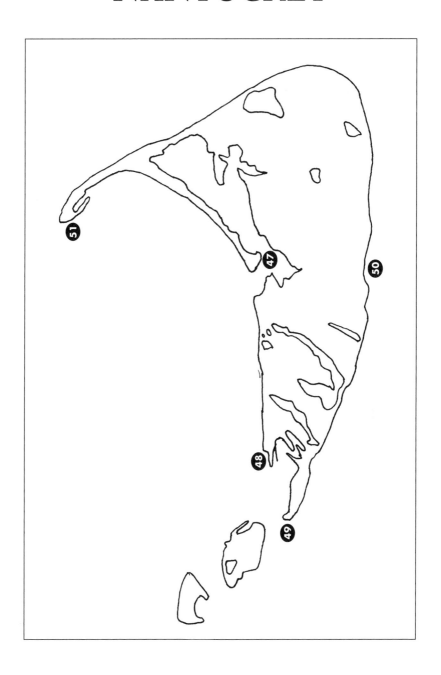

Nantucket

The tendency to group the offshore islands of Nantucket and Martha's Vineyard is without basis. All similarity ends after addressing the fact that they are both islands. Nantucket is more distinctive, slightly more exclusive, and certainly farther to sea. Comparisons between the two crop up incessantly. I would never dare publicly take a position as to which had the better surfcasting. The one arbitrary call I am tempted to make is that there are more bluefish, bonito, and albacore on Nantucket than anywhere else, and this is because of the isle's proximity to the Gulf Stream, which gives it access to more tropical species and lengthens its season.

While nervously plodding the gangway ashore, it's hard to avoid the sense of having come to some strange and distant place. Dedication to fishing oozes from every cultural cue: Well-manicured charter vessels crowd the docks to serve those willing to fish for just anything; and there are just enough buggies—fly rods on the roof racks—sprinkled amid the busy streets to prove that there are still some people who know exactly what they are fishing for and that surfcasting is alive and well on Nantucket.

Unique to Nantucket is the fact that four out of five hot spots required the use of a buggy. Yet Brant Point, where one is not needed, was rated four by me—even though everyone I spoke to about it gave it five. I simply could not put Brant Point up there with Montauk or Plum Island.

47
Brant Point
Nantucket, Massachusetts

BEST MONTHS TO FISH: June through October.
RECOMMENDED METHODS: Live bait and fly fishing.
FISH YOU CAN EXPECT TO CATCH: Stripers.
HOW TO GET THERE: From the ferry dock, take a right onto South Beach, then right onto Easton Street. Officials are sensitive about illegal parking, so park up near the rotary.

When arriving by ferry, Brant Point is just about the first thing you see. It is the picturesque lighthouse on the west side (right) of the harbor opening. Tradition and experience dictate that the only thing to use here is chunk bait: whole bunkers and mackerel, and if the live article is not available, drifted dead; or live eels. The big attraction of this spot is that while strong currents are common here, the ferry, when it turns, reverses one engine and powers the other in a routine that drills an 18- to 35-foot-deep hole—only casting distance from shore. Moreover, bait is forced closer to the protected beach by the periodic action of ferry arrivals.

Chances of a 40- or 50-pounder are better here than anywhere else on Nantucket, and nights are best because of reduced boat traffic. Immediately west of the point there is excellent fly fishing on the flats and on the sandbar inside the west jetty. Timing is the lower drop, mid-tide down. You don't need a buggy to fish here. This is a quality rather than quantity spot. You come here with a single mission in mind: Mr. Big.

CONTACT TIP: Bill Pew of Fisher's Tackle, (508) 228-2261, has the Nantucket story.

48
Eel Point/Knuckles (Dionis)
Nantucket, Massachusetts

BEST MONTHS TO FISH: June through October.
RECOMMENDED METHODS: Plugs and fly fishing.
FISH YOU CAN EXPECT TO CATCH: Stripers and bluefish.
HOW TO GET THERE: Turn west from Main Street onto Madaket Road, then take a right onto Eel Point Road; at land's end, turn left (west). (Over-sand vehicle necessary.)

This largely protected sand beach area is on the north shore of the west end. Extensive shallows that wind around the bend of Eel Point and into Madaket Harbor provide a bait-holding feature and the opportunity for wading vast flats that often hold good numbers of stripers in the deep of night. This "flat water" fishing appeals particularly to the army of new saltwater fly fishers at Nantucket. Spared from an eastern exposure, it is a great spot for escaping the early part of any impending storm. Of course, there are blues here, but they are decidedly secondary to the stripers.

The top two hours of the tide are popular at Eel Point. Remember also that here a humping sou'west, though in your face, will bring activity close in to the beach. Locals call all of this area Dionis, but that can lead to confusion for us outsiders, because the real fishing is on the west, toward Eel Point, not at the Dionis Beach where they bathe in shallows that are not the basis for this spot's reputation among surfcasters.

CONTACT TIP: For a second opinion call Barry Thurston's Tackle Shop, (508) 228-9595.

Islanders rush to Smith Point.

49
Smith Point
Nantucket, Massachusetts

BEST MONTHS TO FISH: May through November.
RECOMMENDED METHODS: Plug fishing and some fly fishing.
FISH YOU CAN EXPECT TO CATCH: Stripers and bluefish.

HOW TO GET THERE: Turn west from Main Street onto Madaket Road, then take a right onto Ames Avenue; at a dirt crossing, turn right for the beach. (Over-sand vehicle recommended.)

This sou'west-facing corner of the island usually enjoys gentle onshore winds and a steady dole of currents; both sweep the island and Madaket Harbor. At Smith Point proper, there is always a strong tide rip leaving the shore. This is a popular spot that often collects anglers for reasons that are obvious to any striper zealot, but wait— there's more: The protected, more estuarine Madaket flats appeal to fly rodders and Rebel, Red Fin, and other light plugcasters. From the beach access road out to the point, a distance of about 2 miles, you will see any number of bars and holes that invite serious surfcasters to exercise their beach-reading skills. Some of these spots enjoy local names and draw good numbers of anglers. While plug fishing the open beach is the most popular, there is some bait fishing both very early and very late in the season. June and October are the prime months for migrating stripers to visit the island. In between, stray stripers and a late July onslaught of bluefish keep things interesting. A rising tide has an edge here, but right at Smith Point there is a good rip on the falling tide as well. The area where buggies come onto the beach can be fished without a buggy.

CONTACT TIP: Bill Pew of Fisher's Tackle, (508) 228-2261.

50

Surfside Beach (Miacomet Pond)
Nantucket, Massachusetts

BEST MONTHS TO FISH: June through October.
RECOMMENDED METHODS: Plugs.

FISH YOU CAN EXPECT TO CATCH: Stripers and bluefish.

HOW TO GET THERE: Take Surfside Road south from town to land's end. Travel west on the beach from there. (Oversand vehicle required.)

East of the Smith Point beach area, or, if you cut left when going for Smith, the nearly 4-mile stretch of south shore can be read and worked to the max. I say that because this is where people who know their striper P's and Q's like to go a-huntin'. They apply their previous knowledge of the local shore, read the beach, and use a system of probing—a cast here and a cast there. Besides cliffs that prevent easy access by foot, the sand along here can be soft as well as washed out. Thus, any beach-buggy operator should be experienced in over-sand operation. Because the sands shift on a year-to-year basis, it is a location where you can lose a vehicle. It's no place to start out developing skills. Like Smith Point, prevailing winds keep this a reasonably safe spot. Incoming water is more popular, but, as I've learned elsewhere, anytime one tide is good, the other is never half bad. Good chase-me, catch-me running the beach in fall up to early November.

CONTACT TIP: You can try calling either Bill Pew of Fisher's Tackle, (508) 228-2261, or Barry Thurston's Tackle Shop, (508) 228-9595, for any of the Nantucket locations. They both know.

51
Great Point
Nantucket, Massachusetts

BEST MONTHS TO FISH: July through October.

RECOMMENDED METHODS: Surface poppers, which are often chosen for casting qualities.

FISH YOU CAN EXPECT TO CATCH: Bluefish, stripers, and occasional bonito.

HOW TO GET THERE: Go east out of town on either Orange or Pleasant streets, both of which become Milestone Road, on which you travel a short distance. Go left onto Polpis Road. Continue for 3½ miles until you arrive at a left turn for Wauwinet Road. Here you'll come upon a gate house operated by the reservation trustees where they sell beach-vehicle permits, maps, and regulations for Great Point. (Over-sand vehicle required.)

Reaching out from the northeast corner of the island, Great Point is a collision center for a dozen currents that don't have a clue where they are going. This mass confusion of water is often clapping into the sky (depending on the wind) and producing a tide rip one is not likely to forget. It has to be one of the most visually stimulating surfcasting spots in this book. In season, it seems that there are always bluefish to be caught, regardless of tide or time of day. Daylight hours often enjoy a greater popularity, as surfcasters find it such a welcome novelty to fish in a world where they can see.

With blues the number-one quarry, the game here is casting a surface popper as far as you can, not only to cover more water, but also to splash through a patch of surface that the fellow beside you can't reach. Consequently, Polaris, Roberts Casting Plugs, and the native (and famous) Nantucket Rabbit—all designed to throw a mile now and catch later—dominate techniques. Light lines on large spools, which deplete less on the cast, are used by some to extend their range. On occasion, some opportunists, bored with conventional methods, might reach for a fly rod when action is close.

Of course, if it's on Nantucket, it's got to be a striper spot at some point, and Great Point does have its striper nights—probably

June and October. But striper fishing from shore is not what gives the point its place of honor. (It lost one in its rating because of that.) Similarly, anyone coming here in the hope of beaching a bonito is apt to be disappointed. Nevertheless, although such an event is rare at any shore location, it is statistically more likely to happen here than elsewhere.

CONTACT TIP: Bill Pew of Fisher's Tackle, (508) 228-2261, or Barry Thurston's Tackle Shop, (508) 228-9595.

CAPE COD CANAL

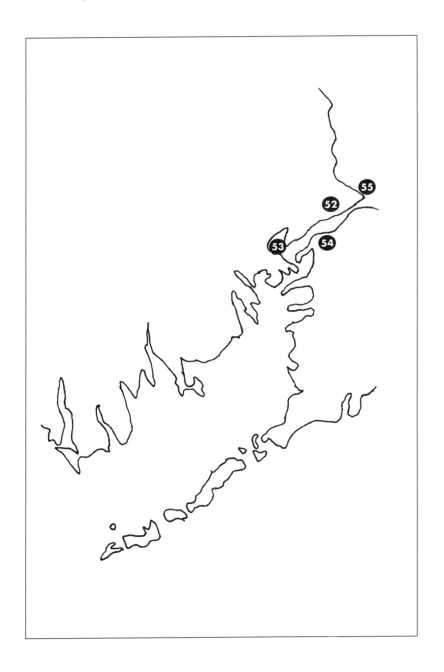

Cape Cod Canal

At just under 8 miles long, and averaging 600 feet wide, the Cape Cod Canal, which was planned to accommodate vessels drafting less than 30 feet, offers more productive striper spots for its area than any other location on the Striper Coast. Indeed, the four hot spots listed here are intended only to represent dozens more unlisted Canal locations, because I dare not consume too many pages of this work with the Canal alone. The result, were I to do so, would be boring duplication. How many times can I say the same things when listing the "Portigy Hole," Aptuxit, Jungle, Cribin, or Murderer's Row, to name only some? The methods and conditions for them are so similar that they would only further mire all efforts to avoid repetitiveness. I prefer to treat those that are unique in the numbered sections and utilize this general introduction for a broad discussion of the Canal's shore fishing. For instance, in every Canal spot where surfcasters gather, chunks of bunker or mackerel, fresh or frozen, are fished on the bottom. This method is currently state-of-the-art Canal fishing and begs a certain amount of social interpretation.

In my life on the Striper Coast, I have witnessed profound transitions in angling methods everywhere, but nowhere have they been as drastic as here. Thirty years ago, the Canal was frequented by a highly sophisticated, esoteric group of hard-cores who believed in fishing with the rod in hand and casting artificials. Then, they "skinned" the Canal by throwing eel-skin rigs that were hollow, cast well, and sank to strike-inducing depths. Making behavioral observations about striper movements and problem solving were accepted aspects of the sport. Today, a high percentage—though certainly not all—of Canal anglers are content to wait beside a chunk-baited rod. Those who do this, and I have no problem with it, will argue that chunking is what works best. I submit, however, that this is a case of self-fulfilling prophecy. If there is a failing to this kind of baitfishing, it is that it fails to cover water and it lacks mobility.

Many of the old-time Canal surfcasters used a bicycle, complete with bumper spikes similar to those on a buggy, to travel the tow roads along the banks. Such sense and innovation was their way of dealing with rules forbidding motor vehicles. That kind of enthusiasm is rare today. To spot cast to breaking fish chasing whiting, serious anglers carried a stack of rods. If a plug fell off the mark of a breaking fish, the caster needed only to drop the first stick and let fly with another. Such target work with repeating weapons saves time. Most important, these methods were the product of well-thought-out fishing strategies. But the door swings both ways: the rocket scientists of the time were not smart enough to fly fish.

But if this contrast between generations teaches us anything, it is that a whole new legion of virgin surfcasters is coming along, most of them born of the recovery of striped bass as a viable gamefish in the late eighties. Some of them will bring something new, and others will stick doggedly to tradition, while the wiser ones will draw from the best of both worlds.

The Cape Cod Canal of thirty years ago was a well-known hot spot of the Striper Coast. In the interim, however, the place fell out of favor, killing a couple of old-time tackle shops in the process and proving that just about everything on this planet is destined to repeat a cycle of ups and downs. We need only tip a curious head in observation in order to recognize the rediscovery of the Canal, even chuckle over the whispered praises uttered excitedly anyplace where surfcasters gather, to appreciate that we have gone full circle there in our devotions at the altar of striper fishing.

52

Herring Run
Cape Cod Canal, Bourne, Massachusetts

BEST MONTHS TO FISH FOR STRIPERS: Late May, early June, October.

RECOMMENDED METHODS: Any large silvery artificial.

FISH YOU CAN EXPECT TO CATCH: Big stripers.

HOW TO GET THERE: Take Route 25 to exit 2 (Bourne); then, from the rotary, follow Route 6 east along the north bank of the Canal for 2¼ miles. It is the first slightly developed area you will see—parking, a motel and shore food—fried clams, clam cakes, fries.

The Cape Cod Canal Herring Run is a small stream that empties into the Canal at a state park on Route 6. Alewives, which are an anadromous fish engaged in a spawning run that begins in early April, run upstream until early June, and spent fish—those coming back downstream to the sea—drop back until mid-June. Also known locally as "herring," these 8–10 inch silvery baitfish provide foraging opportunities acting as a draw for spring migrating stripers.

Time was when anglers took advantage of this situation by dip-netting the herring and live-lining them with a hook in their body. That is no more because so many herring were being taken as bait, and coupled with the commercial removal of them for baiting lobster pots, the pressure was so great that it threatened the continuation of the run. Natural fisheries like this one, which have gone on for hundreds of years, are too valuable to be lost to careless overfishing. It is now illegal to use the herring/alewives for bait. Consequently, the need to use alternative fishing methods that are way less effective has reduced this hot spot from four fish to one fish. You can still fish there but with so many real herring for stripers to compare to your relative junk, you are not likely to do as well. To me having bass slurping baitfish while you throw artificial herring in the form of rubber shads or big wood swimmers is an exercise in frustration. Your chances are better fishing where the competition is a little lighter. This was once a high-profile spot with plenty of parking, restrooms, and picnic tables. It is worth seeing even if you don't choose to fish there because it is cool to see all those fish zooming and jumping up the fishways like small salmon.

The first keepable stripers are usually caught around May 20, and the really large brutes, say around 40 pounds, June 1, give or take. The later in the season, the better the whoppertunity for a big fish until the herring are gone mid-June. You can take bass during the day here but the night is still better.

In the fall, when the young-of-the-year alewives are dropping downstream for return to the sea, their presence would have to draw south-migrating stripers as this happens all over the Striper Coast at any place where there are juvenile spawn-outs. Anytime you are passing this spot, the wise angler should check it out for stripers pigging on the little buggers.

All regulations evolve and we can only treat this hot spot on the basis of what is in place at press time. Perhaps, once the run is restored to suitable levels that can sustain themselves, some sort of relaxation for the taking of bait might come into play. With live-lining herring, we rated it four fish. Now, using artificials, it is one fish.

CONTACT TIP: Call the old and reliable Red Top Sporting Goods at (508) 759-3371. I've called them and when it is bad they say so—a good thing.

53
Massachusetts Maritime Academy
Cape Cod Canal, Bourne, Massachusetts

BEST MONTHS TO FISH: June through October.
RECOMMENDED METHODS: Swimming plugs and fly fishing.
FISH YOU CAN EXPECT TO CATCH: Stripers and bluefish.
HOW TO GET THERE: From Main Street in Bourne, turn south, toward the Canal, at the traffic light onto Academy Drive.

Massachusetts Maritime Academy is located on the north bank at the west end. Here the Canal widens and eddies, causing the currents to subside where pockets of slower water act as a haven for bait. Thus, while gamefish can pass you at any point in the "ditch," they are more likely to stop in this area. Also, unlike most of the rest of the Canal, it is shallow enough to do some wading, with suitable room for the backcast of a fly fisher. Among more traditional methods, small plugs tied direct to simulate sperling work well in the deep of night. The last two hours of the dropping tide are my favorites here.

The section of Canal bank belonging to the Academy is closed to parking from 10:00 P.M. to 6:00 A.M.; it is possible, however, to tuck one's vehicle elsewhere and walk the tow road for areas east of there that share the same shoreline characteristics.

CONTACT TIP: Call the old and reliable Red Top Sporting Goods at (508) 759-3371 or Maco's Bait and Tackle, (508) 759-9836, can help you.

54

Mud Flats (Tidal Flats Recreational Area)
Cape Cod Canal, Bourne, Massachusetts

BEST MONTHS TO FISH: June through October.

RECOMMENDED METHODS: Plugs, chunks, live eels, jigs, and fly fishing.

FISH YOU CAN EXPECT TO CATCH: Stripers and bluefish.

HOW TO GET THERE: After crossing the Bourne Bridge (Route 28), take a right onto Trowbridge Road from the rotary. At the next intersection, take a right onto Shore Road. Watch on your right for Bell Road, which leads to a pair of Corps of Engineers parking areas.

The Mud Flats, as they are fondly known by Canal regulars, are a departure from usual Canal banks, as there is a cove at the west end of this area. During high tide, bait gathers and gamefish will come in to take it. Once the tide starts dropping, it is possible to follow an imaginary line—it would be a continuation of the Canal bank—out on the flats for better plug casting or fly-fishing opportunities in both directions. Of course, surfcasters are taking a chance here when they venture out too soon in deep-of-night striper fishing. Too far left into the cove is already dangerous, but too far right toward the Canal can be deadly. Listen to your fears; allow the tide to drop a little more each time when you begin here, and go out behind someone who has done it before. Once comfortable with flats-wading in the night, you will recognize that an early arrival to the west, or far end, of the flats can produce opportunities for the hungriest and greatest number of stripers. At the shore end, dry with the usual Canal rocky shore, many like to fish a menhaden or mackerel chunk on the bottom; some will bounce worms on the bottom.

CONTACT TIP: Call Red Top Sporting Goods at (508) 759-3371 or Maco's Bait and Tackle, (508) 759-9836, can help you.

The Canal's east end leads in popularity, but there is much more.

55
East End (Scusset)
Cape Cod Canal, Sandwich, Massachusetts

BEST MONTHS TO FISH: July through September.
RECOMMENDED METHODS: Big plugs, chunks, and fly fishing.
FISH YOU CAN EXPECT TO CATCH: Stripers.

HOW TO GET THERE: From the north rotary of the Sagamore Bridge, where Routes 6 and 3 intersect, follow signs east to Scusset Beach. Park as deep and as far right as you can to be near the Canal.

Just about all the stripers that summer in Cape Cod Bay will show up, sooner or later, lounging in the currents of the east end of the Canal. Longtime regulars will tell you that the rule is to be at this end during east, or falling, tides; however, the system works best when the tide is falling through the dawn. What that means is that a Boston high tide of 11:00 P.M. to midnight, which will have water flowing east during the dawn, is an excellent starting point for anyone hoping to intercept a moby striper on a feeding safari. Once the water begins to slow down, however, the fishing is over. During those seasons, when there are good populations of whiting or squid, it is possible to witness the awesome force of a big bass beating the surface of the Canal in pursuit of breakfast. The first time I saw it, I thought a mule had been dropped from the Sagamore Bridge.

Use highly castable, overweight swimmers—such as loaded Atoms, Dannys, or Pikies—during the darkened hours and keep an ear cocked for the sound of thrashing fish. Once first light is in evidence, shift to poppers that will reach as far into the ditch as possible. Reverse Atoms, Gibbs Polaris, and oversized Striper Swipers should be used not only for their castability but also for their size. The trick here is to spot-cast a feeding fish as quickly as possible. Speed and accuracy count! Old standbys such as floater Rebels, with or without teasers, or 9-inch Slug-Gos will take those that are already in range.

Climb down the rocks beneath the last amber Canal light, then walk the sandy shore east beneath the breakwater; at this stage of the tide—low at dawn—the water is shallow enough to both pass and wade comfortably. Regulars will set up to fish the bottom with chunks just east of the rocky shoal under the light. Pluggers and fly fishers can wade east of there and still be in excellent water.

CONTACT TIP: Call Red Top Sporting Goods at (508) 759-3371 or Maco's Bait and Tackle, (508) 759-9836, can help you.

MAINLAND
MASSACHUSETTS

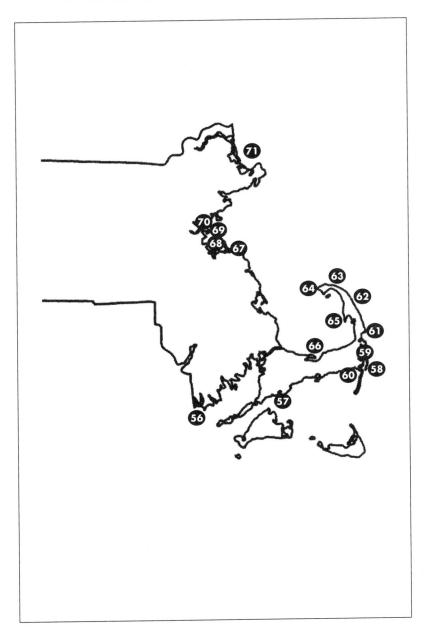

Mainland Massachusetts

As the geographic center of the Striper Coast, Massachusetts leads the list of striper states by any measurement you choose. It offers the highest level of striper fishing, because it is most suitably situated to intercept the migration routes of both races of linesides—those of the Hudson and of the Chesapeake. It combines an enhanced level of access with a suitable coastline for holding linesides. Moreover, opportunities for other species certainly match, if not exceed, those found elsewhere. In addition to yielding Charles Church's All-Tackle World Record, which held for over fifty years, the Bay State boasts more 70-pound-plus striper landings than any other. Besides mainland Massachusetts, the Canal, Cape, and islands combine to offer the shore fisherman twenty-eight hot spots. Needless to say, if I could have only one striper state, this would be it.

Those of us who study the influence of environment on fishing know that there are two sets of climatic conditions in Massachusetts, where water temperatures can be dramatically different. By midsummer, the Gulf of Maine and Nantucket Sound are reading a difference of ten degrees or more, a factor that plays no small part in the determination of arrivals and departures of all marine species. For the shore fisherman, the line of temperature gradient occurs on either side of Monomoy Island, on the southeast corner of Cape Cod. Because of these differences, it is possible to frolic in the tepid waters of Nantucket Sound at seventy degrees in August while your counterpart is chipping his teeth in the suds of Nauset Beach—5 miles east as the gull flies—where the water is in the mid-fifties. Thus, north-shore striper arrivals and departures are trimmed by two or more weeks at each end of the season.

But the Bay State is not all buttercups and breezes: witness, for example, the death of Cape Cod surf fishing. Under the guise of "management," the Cape Cod National Seashore caretakes the entire Outer Cape under a closure (imposed in 1985) that prohibits use of an over-sand vehicle on the beaches there for all but 7 of 47 miles. Under this management plan, it is impossible to carry equipment the vast distances involved, let alone carry a fish out.

With one exception, I didn't include other south shore locations on the Cape, because any that might exist would do so in the milieu of better opportunities on the major beaches and Cape Cod Canal. Why fish Bass River when you can have the Canal? Except for Hull Gut, the stretch from North River to Boston is fraught with problems that reflect the same hardening of access so common in and around cities. All the towns on the North River maintain a complicated system of parking stickers limited to residents. Plymouth's Duxbury Beach didn't survive the cut because of environmental considerations. The north bank of the Merrimack River mouth, which is Salisbury Beach, has a productive jetty, but it, too, is overwhelmed by Plum Island. Inside, along the Merrimack River, it is possible to wade and explore the marsh areas very close to the Badger Rocks, a well-known boat-fishing hot spot; next is "Butler's Toothpick," a popular navigation aid that keeps stripermen busy. This inner-river section is quiet enough to hear feeding gamefish at night, and it is possible to wade the flats with small plugs or fly-fishing gear; there are no parking hassles, as the lot at Salisbury Beach State Reservation is open to anglers. In late spring, a good run of better-sized stripers make their way up the Merrimack River chasing alewives. When it was legal, I have seen Lawrence anglers cashing in there, drifting the "herring" the same way they once did in the Canal. But these spots just can't hold up against the Bay State's other offers. We have to draw the line somewhere.

Recent restrictions on the use of alewives or herring, along with their use as a bait, have been promulgated to preserve the runs all over New England. Thus, an evolution in angling methods continues.

56

Westport River Area
Westport, Massachusetts

BEST MONTHS TO FISH: May through November.
RECOMMENDED METHODS: Plugging, live bait, and fly fishing.
FISH YOU CAN EXPECT TO CATCH: Stripers and bluefish.
HOW TO GET THERE: East of Fall River on Route 195, pick up Route 88 south.

The Westport River area is a composite of several spots that seem to have been largely forgotten by the angling world. They are the Westport River, Horseneck Beach, Gooseberry Neck, and Allen's Pond.

About a mile before the shore, where the Route 88 bridge crosses the Westport River, there is a boat-launching ramp on the right. A canoe can be paddled upstream just minutes from that ramp to an island where stripers often gather in the deep night. This is a highly protected estuary where the only hazards are the strong currents of the river and the wake created by boat traffic. In late May and early June, I have taken a number of twentyish stripers there on dead alewives. Moreover, because of the riverine nature of the water here, it is an excellent spot to fly fish.

Between the bridge and the open coast, as you proceed down 88, you will notice on the right the dunes that flank Horseneck State Beach. Here you will find a veritable garden of bass-frequenting holes and bars stretching over 2 miles from the causeway to Gooseberry Island on the east, and to Cherry Point, which guards the mouth of the Westport River, on the west. Cherry Point is a great spot on either tide, but I believe the drop has a slight edge. Access problems, however, rear their heads at Horseneck. While there is a road along the river that leads to Cherry Point, it is blocked and parking is prohibited. Similarly, there is no after-hours parking at Horseneck State Beach, which has spacious parking areas for bathers during the day. Again, as is so much the case throughout the Striper Coast, the access problems are worse in summer. With an over-sand vehicle, I have driven Horseneck Beach in late fall when nobody cares. Horseneck Beach is one of those out-of-the-way spots that is largely forgotten.

Gooseberry Neck, at the east end of Horseneck, reaches seaward, forming a natural barrier. At the sou'west corner of Gooseberry, low tide, there is a nice mix of sandy bottom and rocky shore where stripers and blues seem always to gather. As you look west, you quickly realize that anything moving along the shore has to round this spot on its way to the Cape and islands. And, as is so often the case, positive influences can combine to make a great spot phenomenal. When you add an onshore sou'west—the prevailing summer wind—to a setting sun or rising moon and low tide, the results can be explosive. As this is state property, the only access problem is driving, because the causeway is blocked some years, or damaged by storms, forcing anglers to walk in.

If you go east where Route 88 bumps the shoreline, the shore road—East Beach Road—soon heads back inland, north. To the east, you'll see a collection of summer cottages that influence parking and access to Allen's Pond outflow. You'll see an estuarine backwater that fills and empties with the sea through a break in the beach. Other than some private property among the cottages, the area is now owned and managed by the Massachusetts Audubon Society as the Allen's Pond Wildlife Sanctuary, providing parking for observing wildlife. The location of the outflow, presently about ¾ mile east of Horseneck Road, is always moving but if open, the exchange of water draws stripers particularly on the dropping tide. The opening to this pond lures gamefish all season. The difficulty of access to Allen's Pond varies from time to time.

Back at the mouth of the Westport River, the Acoaxet Rocks guard the west bank of the river entrance. From these rocks, one can easily see Cherry Point and Horseneck Beach a few hundred yards away, but to drive around the west branch of the river by road is 14 miles. Still, during the off-season for tourism, when locals are not around to complain about your parking, that west side of the river opening can host some moby stripers. My first 50-pound-plus lineside was taken there.

CONTACT TIP: Call Westport Marine, (508) 636-8100, for information.

57
South Cape Beach
Mashpee, Cape Cod, Massachusetts

BEST MONTH TO FISH FOR STRIPERS: Late April through October.

RECOMMENDED METHODS: Sea worms on the bottom out front, eels and flies in the back.

FISH YOU CAN EXPECT TO CATCH: Stripers, blackfish (tautog), bluefish.

HOW TO GET THERE: From the intersection of Route 28 and Route 151, Pine Tree Corner in Mashpee, take Great Neck Road—which later becomes Great Oak Road—south for about four miles. Watch for signs for South Cape Beach State Park to assure you are on course. Once at the shore, there is a parking area for accessing South Cape Beach, which is a newly minted Massachusetts state park.

I think of this hot spot in three parts—the front beach, the jetty to the west, and the back pond—which will be the order that we will confront the nuances of the fishing here. For some reason the front beach here is one of the earliest locations for catching the first spring schoolies arriving from the south. Season depending, it is possible to feel the jiggle of a school striper as early as mid-April. Best way to deal with these first arrivals is to put a fresh, live sea worm on the bottom with a sinker. However, the downside of this early activity is that it is a rare striper that is any longer than 20 inches. With today's striper regs a keeper is about impossible this early. But any shortage in size is compensated for by the great numbers of fish. It is not until mid-May that you can expect beach one large enough to bring home. A couple of weeks after the first school stripers there is always a tautog run and the saying here is that if you are bored with school stripers and suddenly hook something taking drag off of your reel you have a delicious tautog or blackfish.

Once the season is going, surfcasters can walk a mile west out onto Dead Neck for fishing the break in the jetty. Experience teaches that the dropping tide is best because of the outflow from Waquoit Bay, but I have caught bass in the jetty opening on the incoming tide as well. Here, because of the current, it is best to fish with lures or fly fish because of problems holding bottom with baits. The jetty is a bit of a hodgepodge of stone but we jetty rats are used to that and will do anything for a striped fish.

A short walk inland from the jetty into Waquoit Bay, in the back, there is a nice rip when the tide is rising. This new water draws linesides from the bay for a sniff of what is new on the striper menu. The bottom here is hard mud and sand without any serious threat of falling into deeper water so you can head for the top of your waders toward the navigation buoys. This kind of in-the-back fishing is a great way to cope with the big water of storms but it is so good that I would still go there if the weather was mild. My favorite weapon of bass destruction is a live eel. What I do is cast into the flow of new water on my left and let the eel drift under tension and even feed line for working water as far out into the bay as I can. A similar pattern of casts with either lures or flies, swinging under tension, will also produce takes from bay fish. Late May on it is possible to catch a real cow here and if I was not such an old man, I would have kept this secret for myself, but I have a lot of spots. Just don't tell anybody that you got it from me. *Staizitto.*

CONTACT TIP: Try any of the Cape Cod Canal area bait and tackles: Red Top Sporting Goods at (508) 759-3371 or Maco's Bait and Tackle, (508) 759-9836.

58
Nauset Beach
Orleans, Cape Cod, Massachusetts

BEST MONTHS TO FISH FOR STRIPERS: Late May through early November.
RECOMMENDED METHODS: Bottom fishing with sea worms, plug fishing, live eels and fly fishing.
FISH YOU CAN EXPECT TO CATCH: Stripers and bluefish.
HOW TO GET THERE: Follow the signs on Route 28 in Orleans to Nauset Beach in East Orleans.

Nauset Beach is the most pristine and primitive beach on the entire Striper Coast. Years when the highly changeable structure is at its best, the primordial beauty is magnified by the bars, sloughs and holes that develop the full length of the shore stretching south to the Chatham Inlet opening to Pleasant Bay. Except for a few private

One of the nicest on the Striper Coast, Nauset is a beautiful east-facing beach.

cottages, little on this barrier beach is man-made. Consequently, the landscape is all dunes, dune grass and white sand that is as fine as talcum.

This spot's reputation is based upon beach-buggy use because of the many miles of east-facing ocean beach involved—a number that long term can be quite variable—six to eleven miles—depending upon the placement of the somewhat mobile Chatham Inlet. Oversand Vehicle Permits, costing over $150 and rising, are issued by the town of Orleans, are required, and access is controlled at the north end of the beach in Orleans. You will enter the town of Chatham partway down the beach. As a result the two towns share in the management and policing of the beach. Except for the large, well-paved parking area at the Orleans end, there are no developed roads to the south. The only approach is by beach buggy or by boat across Pleasant Bay, the latter an unlikely option for anyone who should be fishing at night.

With the over-sand permit requirement, it is necessary for your four-wheel-drive vehicle to pass inspection for suitable equipment. Regulations tighten all the time, but in addition to the annual permit there are also daily fees.

The last ten years seals have inhabited the entire Outer Cape in ever-increasing numbers. Because they feed upon fish, it is commonly believed that they are to blame for the slight decline in surfcasting opportunity. While it may be difficult to prove, it does make sense. On the other hand, all the areas of the Striper Coast have always offered inconsistent angling where each hot spot takes its turn at being both memorable then unaccountably dull in its performance. But when a big dark head pops up in your surf during the deep night it can be quite unnerving.

The structure and condition of the beach is the sum total of the preceding month's weather. Consequently, in some seasons there is little structure to appeal to stripers, while in others, holes and ditches mark more hot spots than can be fished in a night. As a rule the shallower holes are vacated at low tide, though linesides will return to them as soon as they have enough water for cover. Deeper spots of course will hold fish the tide around. In the bigger holes tide has less meaning, and at high tide, structure is obscure, impossible to read, and less confining for the linesides feeding there. Thus, while fish can be in, they can be anywhere. A good rule is that the more extreme the structure, the more likely it is to host fish. It is also important to treat each hole edge as a separate item. Often, bass will hang on the north or south edge because of how the water sweeps over. One has to test these places to determine how the bite is taking place. The buggers can drive you crazy.

One reliable hole where structure is most likely to build to productive levels regularly from year to year is Pochet Hole, which is at the first opening in the dune track going left or east when coming on. This is only a mile south of the beach access where a non-four-wheel-drive can be parked if you are not using a buggy. A person can walk that distance and have private fishing the whole mile along the way, free of vehicles, which are restricted to the back track out of sight. Moreover, their lights are not able to spook fish from the shallow wash because of the dune height between their track and your shore. It's mouse quiet and stripers like that.

The discussion brings to mind that while Nauset Beach is a four-fish rating using a beach-buggy, it is still at least a two fish for surfcasters on foot who park few, if any, cars in the thousand-car parking lot free during the night. You can walk the beach alone, examine the structure, listen for the slurps of bass swilling on sand eels, look at the stars and be thankful such places still exist. Moreover, north the other way from the parking lot, it gets even nicer when you get to Gorilla Hole where big boulders—the only rocks on the Outer Cape—mark the beginning of even better fishing.

When talking about the best surfcasting on the Striper Coast, it is necessary to break up this entire area according to its geographical character. You will notice that hot spots run into each other both in their proximity and similarity. The Outer Cape is a region that is too large and diverse in its fishing to be combined in its parts.

CONTACT TIP: To find out what locals are saying about Nauset Beach, call The Hookup in Orleans, (508) 240-0778.

59
Chatham Inlet (North Edge, on Nauset Beach)
Chatham, Cape Cod, Massachusetts

BEST MONTHS TO FISH FOR STRIPERS: June through November.
RECOMMENDED METHODS: Plugs, live and rigged eels, fly fishing.
FISH YOU CAN EXPECT TO CATCH: Stripers and blues.
HOW TO GET THERE: Follow the signs on Route 28 in Orleans to Nauset
   Beach in East Orleans. Drive the full length of the beach south to
   the end. (Over-sand vehicle required.)

At the south end of Nauset Beach there is usually an opening into
Pleasant Bay. It has to be said that way because Nauset Beach has
always been defined and bordered by the inlet opening within the
town of Chatham. For at least 50 years prior to 1987, the "Inlet"
evolved through a slow, 100-foot-per-year, migration southward
toward Monomoy Island. But no object or collection of material can
be stretched indefinitely without failure at some point and during the
early January nor'easter of 1987 the sea broke through the overly thin
barrier beach, creating a new inlet to Pleasant Bay while shortening
the barrier beach by roughly four miles. Since this destructive
storm, the inlet area of influence has undergone dramatic changes
in placement, flow, and opening width. A consequence fishing-wise
is that changes in water flow and angling opportunity have become
highly changeable. Thus, we are relegated to speculation about
what you might find there during the particular year you are fishing.
Traditionally, this inlet has been able to draw excellent numbers of
stripers and bluefish on both of its sides, all the years that it is there
without regard for its particular placement. But angling on the north

side has characteristics that are somewhat different than those on the south.

All three forms of Chatham Inlet that I have fished, the north edge has offered good fishing on the incoming tide about as soon as there is enough water to cover a striper's back after dark. Early in the rise, bass are drawn up from the depths of Pleasant Bay. Later, mid-tide on, fish will enter the inlet from the outside along Nauset Beach. Some nights there are big water sweeps, which can be dangerous if they are too pushy on surfmen. As a rule, and the beach nomenclature is changing all the time, you'll be working the currents from a bar end with a deep drop-off on the bay side. Whatever the situation might be when you get there, generalizations about a best time are difficult to rely on. Just when you think you have the place figured out, fish show up when they are not supposed to. Time was when 8:00 to 10:00 P.M. high tides on the Boston tide chart (the adjustment from Boston to Chatham is only minutes) were the most reliable. Autumn, when days are shorter, productive evening tides can start as early as 6:00 P.M. Whether or not that is still the case is up to speculation but it is a good starting point. Slack tide at the inlet mouth is another good time to be fishing. It seems that the musical chairs of changing position takes place so eat your lunch at another time.

Popular methods here are plug and fly fishing because the currents are too strong for holding bottom baits. The Finnish genre of swimmer—Rebels, Red Fins, Rapalas, Mambos, Nils-Masters, Bombers—are a staple. You are safer with the bigger models, and never hesitate to employ the traditional big wood—Pikies, Dannys and Atom swimmers your uncle left you. Nights when the bass are picky, use the smaller models of swimmer. The first bluefish should not show until late July.

Because of the distance down the beach from the Orleans parking lot, roughly six miles, don't even think of fishing here without a beach buggy. There are enough good places in the region where that is not necessary. Another degradation of the fishing here is that some years the National Park Service closes sections or even all of the beach in order not to disturb nesting shorebirds. Also keep in mind that seals hang out where the fish hang out and the fish are here.

CONTACT TIP: Blackbeards, (508) 240-3369.

60
Chatham Inlet, South Side—Chatham Light Beach
Chatham, Cape Cod, Massachusetts

BEST MONTHS TO FISH FOR STRIPERS: May to November.
RECOMMENDED METHODS: Plugs, live eels, fly fishing.
FISH YOU CAN EXPECT TO CATCH: Stripers and blues.
HOW TO GET THERE: Follow the signs on Route 28 in Chatham to Chatham Light. Park in the lot across the street from the Coast Guard Station where the lighthouse is located. You can see the beach and inlet to the east.

As with the north lip of Chatham Inlet on Nauset Beach, this hot spot was formed by the great northeaster of 1987 and continues to be vulnerable enough to storms for a lot of change. The opening moves, the depth changes, and the width of the opening vary as a response to the depth and the inlet's influence upon passing gamefish on the Cape's outside. So far there has always been some kind of opening that permits new seawater to refresh Pleasant Bay. Were it to close as the result of some anomalies in tide or weather, officials would keep it open so as to provide for shellfish survival in the bay and ocean access for the local commercial fishing fleet. So there will always be something here that will lure gamefish. Because of the new position of the inlet, an "island" is left on the south side, which really connects to the mainland. Today it is possible to walk across new sand to the south edge of Chatham Inlet or even fish the east-facing South Island beach. Keep in mind that even if not fishing the inlet proper, all adjacent waters remain under the inlet's influence. In spite of similarities and shared waters, it is necessary to treat the south side of the inlet opening separately because of unique legal and geographic limitations, which are markedly different. For example, not only is it not necessary to use a buggy here, it is not allowed. Secondly, this side of Chatham Inlet enjoys deeper water and, consequently, a greater flow. Most anglers feel that the surfcasting is better here, and all agree that it is certainly more accessible. The best tidal considerations are different too.

Plan for a low tide that occurs during darkened hours and expect to make contact with stripers one hour either side of low tide on the Boston chart. One logical explanation for why this timing is so reliable is that at high tide the inlet opening is ten times the width that it is when the tide is low. This permits gamefish to be anywhere in the half mile opening with ten feet of water over their backs. At low tide, on the other hand, the opening is so much smaller that it restricts gamefish to a much smaller confine that is on the south side of the inlet where you are fishing. As is the case with all inlets, there is a lag between slack low in the Pleasant Bay mouth and the low sea tide—a little over an hour.

Regulars cast plugs across current, permitting them to drift and swim under tension. You can drift a live eel into the faces of gamefish holding in the currents. For better water column penetration, it is possible to use a jig or small rubber shad. Because of the protected, non-surf water, you can fly fish without a stripping basket. Just be mindful of other anglers downtide if you hook a good fish in these robust currents. About as close as you are going to get to Monomoy where the seals abound, keep clear of the seals here in greater numbers.

CONTACT TIP: Blackbeards, (508) 240-3369.

61
Nauset Inlet
Orleans and Eastham
Cape Cod, Massachusetts

BEST MONTHS TO FISH FOR STRIPERS: May to November; June best.
RECOMMENDED METHODS: Plugs and fly fishing.
FISH YOU CAN EXPECT TO CATCH: Stripers and bluefish.
HOW TO GET THERE: From Route 28 in Orleans follow the signs to Nauset Beach on Beach Road to East Orleans until you reach the Nauset Beach parking lot. Walk north or left facing the water for 1½ miles to the inlet.

As the inlet that flanks Nauset Beach on its north end, this opening feeds a good-sized bay comprised of Town Cove, Nauset Harbor and Salt Pond Bay. The estuary here is relatively clean and has a large network of salt marsh supporting extensive marine life. Unlike its sister inlet to the south in Chatham, here the opening is more stable. But there are still compelling similarities in that there is abundant flow with largely the same angling methods in use, and widespread favor with low tide in its timing. There are, however, many more bars and holes flanking both sides of Nauset Inlet, particularly the south side, which is covered more extensively here.

Once you begin walking north from the parking lot, you will begin to see improvement in the structure—holes, outer bars and surf-laced rocks. An excellent stretch of water lies just to the north of the Nauset Beach parking lot, an area that is both accessible on foot and free of beach-buggy traffic. Within ¼ mile, you can be fishing surf that is influenced by Nauset Inlet's changeable waters. The large rocks are the only place on all of the Outer Cape where you will find rocks in the surf.

The rocks are at Gorilla Hole and have long been known for their ability to draw and hold big stripers. The further north you go, the better it gets. Many has been the angler bound for the inlet who never got there for the fish found along the way.

Nearer to the inlet, outer bars will be evident at low tide, and it is possible to cross backwaters to reach them. However, all surfmen should listen to their fears, especially in earlier, unfamiliar excursions, because this can be a very unforgiving place to fish. Because of lag, water can be flying out of the inlet, leaving the impression of a dropping tide, when in fact the sea tide out front is rising and closing off your return to the dry beach. Once the tide turns, it is easy to get trapped on one of the higher spots out there, forcing a dangerous crossing that could be over your waders and causing you to wish you had brought your rubber ducky.

Late in the dropping tide, some anglers go in the backwaters behind the dunes toward town in the shadow of Nauset Heights. The falling waters sweep through here and bass will often hold in the current. Their presence can be betrayed by the slurping and popping of the feed bag. And it is a safer place to be than out on the bars blowing air into a beach toy.

The access politics of Nauset Inlet are another of those frustrations that greet surf fishers. For the 40 years that I know of officials have kept outsiders from driving there in ORVs through the hopelessly arbitrary regulation of maintaining the public right-of-way for residents only. Townies have discreetly used an access at Nauset Heights permitted by their resident stickers as a means of excluding outsiders who paid outrageous non-resident beach fees for the rest of Nauset Beach. I have driven there during mid-watch hunts for stripers and have never been kicked out. Nor have I ever heard of anyone brought before the courts for doing so. While I can offer no legal advice, I have doubts than any town can define public with two interpretations. Nauset Inlet is also accessible on its north edge from Coast Guard beach at the National Seashore. At least there no driving is allowed for anybody. Similarly, the walk to the inlet is also about 1½ miles. Parking passes for night parking—when you should be fishing—are issued at the Visitor's Center.

CONTACT TIP: Blackbeards, (508) 240-3369.

62
Outer Cape
Cape Cod National Seashore
Truro/Wellfleet, Massachusetts

BEST MONTHS TO FISH: August through October.
RECOMMENDED METHODS: Plugs, rigged eels, live eels, and fly fishing.
FISH YOU CAN EXPECT TO CATCH: Stripers and bluefish.
HOW TO GET THERE: Going north to Provincetown on Route 6, watch for signs on the right to the various swim beaches.

From High Head clear to the Eastham side of Nauset Inlet, there is a 22-mile stretch of wild beach about which little is commonly known. Here, great bars stretch seaward like fingers; at the corners

Steeped in surfcasting tradition, the Outer Cape commonly hosts moby stripers.

where they meet the beach, there are holes where baitfish gather. At some of the prominent points, depending on the tide, the sea claps up straight where waves collide; along some straight stretches of shore, there are trenches where moby stripers will swim all night looking for something to eat.

At the north end of this magical stretch, Highland Light warns the shipping lanes of impending doom. South of that there is Balston, Newcomb Hollow, LeCount, and Nauset North Beach. It is here that modern-day salvagers have about finished plundering the gold bullion and coin of the *Widah*, a wreck of Spanish origin whose grave has lain just outside the striper bars for 300 years. Here, many of the Cape's great stripers and surfmen have met in battle. This stretch south of Highland Light was the private killing ground of the legendary striperman Arnold Laine, and it was for years Frank Daignault's best-kept secret. This stretch was also the site of much of my autobiography, *Twenty Years on the Cape: My Time as a Surfcaster*.

Parking areas at High Head, Head-of-the-Meadow, Newcomb Hollow, LeCount, and Nauset North Beach are closed at night, but permits for fishing/parking are available at the Visitor's Center on Airport Road in Provincetown. On foot, it is possible to hike in to areas that you've scouted during the day. However, it is imperative that you minimize equipment to enhance mobility: Fish barefoot in summer; use only one rod; have a rope for no more than one fish; keep the plug bag small. Humongous stripers are here.

This is an area where access on foot must be chosen carefully. Many of the dunes are so high, so amorphous, that a person could be buried alive in a descent. Such incidents have been documented. Climbing such dunes in departure is also impossible. Fishing productivity would be enhanced with a beach vehicle, but that has not been allowed since the mid-1980s, when complaints from local pressure groups caused the entire stretch in this listing to be closed to vehicular traffic. On foot, a well-conditioned person could not sample 5 percent of the structure.

Years when it could be driven—the same years when I was a rod-and-reel commercial fisherman—my wife, Joyce, and I fished every hole, every slough, every bar. Stripers that have been rooting for either sand eels or sea worms will often have abrasions on their chin and lips from the sand, telling us how and where we had to fish. We had thousand-dollar nights back when people worked a month for that. No more. But those who can take the demands of this fine stretch of shore will find it worth the effort.

Only one mile of this Outer Cape section is open to off-road vehicles (ORVs)—the section beginning at Long Nook extending north past Highland or Cape Cod Light to an exit/entrance at Head of the Meadow southeast of Coast Guard swim beach. Hours that permit ORV use for this section are for night fishing only—6:00

P.M. to 7:00 A.M. For a more comprehensive explanation of ORV regulation and use, see the next listed Hot Spot, number 63, the Provincelands.

CONTACT TIP: Blackbeards, (508) 240-3369.

Provinceland currents loaded with fish hurry past the Cape tip.

63
Provincelands (Back Beach)
Cape Cod National Seashore
Provincetown/North Truro, Massachusetts

BEST MONTHS TO FISH: June through October.
RECOMMENDED METHODS: Plugs, rigged eels and fly fishing
FISH YOU CAN EXPECT TO CATCH: Stripers and bluefish.

HOW TO GET THERE: As you come north on Route 6, with Provincetown on your left, take a right onto Race Point Road and drive 1½ miles north to the end of the road at the ranger station. Right or east is a dune road that leads to the Back Beach. This area can also be accessed back 2½ miles off of Route 6 by taking a right going north at High Head Road. You'll see a large lake—Pilgrim Lake—on the east side of Route 6 at the turn. At the end of the dirt road that becomes an over-sand route, you can only go left onto the beach trail as the right is closed to ORV use. An over-sand vehicle is necessary.

This is four-wheel-drive country and you won't get 50 feet without a four-wheeler with the tires aired down for additional traction. Moreover, this federal property is strictly managed by the National Park Service for protection of both its visitors and environment. Consequently, an off-road vehicle (ORV) permit is required and they will not issue you one unless you have the required equipment. (Which see.) The annual ORV permits go on sale late March/early April presently at a fee of $150. There is also a seven-day tourist permit priced at $50.

Self-contained Recreational Vehicle (SCV) Permits issued for camper-equipped pickups or chassis-mounted four-wheel-drive vehicles are also issued at the fee of $225 annual (today's prices) and $75 for 7 days. Between July 1 and Labor Day a maximum total of 21 days are allowed for SCV use. The information phone line for station hours, driving conditions, and other information is (508) 487-3698.

Present regulations permit about six miles of front beach driving from Race Point Light to the closure at High Head with only a slight interruption at the swim area in front of the Race Point Ranger Station at Race Point Road's end. However, shorebirds get first dibs on beach access and NPS sees its role here as protection for piping plover and commonly closes off large sections of beachfront during June and July. So throwing a few hundred in beach permits provides no guarantee that you can go on. If one of the shorebirds, and the species also changes from time to time, winks at the other, there goes your vacation on Patti Page's Old Cape Cod. There is more about which I dislike being the messenger.

Late July a mung or red weed, locally known as gunk, inundates the waters of High Head and south. This awful material, which is not pollution and really natural, makes fishing the beach impossible. The Race is always swept clean unless there is a protracted east storm so there is escape. It is thus necessary to add regulations, closures, gunk and fantastic numbers of seals to the list of surfcasting obstructions that lower its rating. For the finest, most untarnished surfcasting in North America it is still worth it.

AT LAST THE FISHING

East of the ranger station at the end of Race Point Road, the sandy beach curves so slowly that a compass is needed to ascertain that you are moving through an arc. On that circle is a continuous series of points stretching four miles to High Head, which is the limit of your beach driving. Each of these points, but particularly the first ones, the ones to the west, have traditionally been fished during the late half of the rising tide.

However, my experience has been that you could catch great stripers in this area without regard for tide. Moreover, it has always seemed to me that the stripers on the Back Beach were larger than those at the Race. Waters moving into and out of Cape Cod Bay can be felt all through this stretch, which approaches the tip of the Cape. Curiously, currents are left to right most of the time at most places here regardless of tide. Many explain it as "back eddying," when water seems to be traveling in any direction that it shouldn't. As a result best wind for this area is sou'west, and the harder the better because the wind combines with the natural rips to make the water pull, which the fish like. What everybody does is travel from one point to another because such spots have shallow fingers of sand where bass and blues can lie downtide in depths to ambush what comes over. Surf fishers like to cast just a few points downtide of straight out and allow their swimmer to drum in the current while it swings. Once they no longer feel the tension, they rush their cast in for another swing.

One of the things that enabled me to wreak havoc upon linesides for the many years that I lived and fished here was our refusal to accept the timing methods that traditional surfcasters used. The rigor of this area was to fish the late incoming tide. We, on the other hand, fished the late part of the falling tide past low and even into the rise, if fishing was holding up and it often did. During these periods you get a chance to see the structure of the beach and store information about where you should be fishing when the water is high. Winds and their direction play a big part in the fishing.

The early part of an east or southeast wind down the beach from the right can crank linesides up into a frenzy. A question of intensity and timing, once the easterlies get to pumping strong for a while, the water dirties up with the gunk from below High Head and becomes no longer fishable. Know when to fold, as they say, and it might be time to sack in.

These Provincelands are the storied shores where much of surf-casting tradition was born and much of the old ways live on. For instance, it is the last stronghold of the conventional or revolving spool reel. Braided lines of unbreakable ratings up to 65-pound test are used here and because of this equipment, the demand for humongous plugs, particularly swimmers, persists. Giant Pikies, Dannys, Atom 40s, Goo-Goo Eyes, the GTS-3, the Reverse Atom, all stuff hard to find in today's tackle shops, are standard weaponry in P-town. You need these big plugs in order to load the pool cue rods and mighty reels. Keep in mind that I'm not talking about ancient history here; this is how it is now.

One reason why I advocate this hot spot is that my wife and four children have all taken monster stripers here. In July of '77, the year of the Great P-town Blitz, Joyce Daignault, a consummate surfcaster of the highest order, landed a 50-pound, 6-ounce monster for which she won the Governor's Cup. What a night. And in addition she has great taste in men.

CONTACT TIP: For information on P-town and the Lower Cape, call Nelson's, (508) 487-0034, on Race Point Road.

ORV EQUIPMENT REQUIREMENTS FOR OVER-SAND DRIVING

Shovel: Heavy-duty shovel equal to a military folding shovel
Towing device: Any of the following that is at least 14 feet long:

Tow Strap—1½ inch
Rope—¾ inch
Chain—⁵⁄₁₆ inch
Cable—¼ inch

Jack: Standard vehicle manufacturer
Jack support board: Wood 10×12×1½ or ¾-inch plywood
Tire pressure gauge: Must register to 5 psi or lower
SCVs and pickup truck campers must also have a fire extinguisher and permanently mounted holding tanks.

64
Race Point
Cape Cod National Seashore
Provincetown, Massachusetts

BEST MONTHS TO FISH: June through October.
RECOMMENDED METHODS: Plug fishing, rigged eels, sand eel baits, and fly fishing.

Dawn blitz at Race Point with all surfcasters up tight with gamefish.

FISH YOU CAN EXPECT TO CATCH: Stripers and bluefish.

HOW TO GET THERE: Follow Route 6, then take a right onto Race Point Road. Turn left, or west, at the ranger station. (Over-sand vehicle recommended.)

Race Point Light, which lies a little over a mile west of the ranger station entrance, is the most reliable hot spot in P-town. There have been periods when stripers were there around the clock, usually when there was a howling sou'west in your face. Thankfully, this is a prevailing wind, because it is almost a requirement for fishing the Race with any success. There have also been times, such as during an east storm, when the Race was hot during the late end of a rising tide. Along with those wind requirements, another safe rule is the good fishing at low tide. Timing-wise, whenever Race Bar was crowded during a dropping tide, fish usually arrived three and a half hours after Boston high tide on the tide chart. It was usually time to quit once the tide was two hours up. I often felt that stripers were still there but that the rising water had backed us up so far that I could no longer reach the positioned fish with my plug. Because the intensity of the fishing is dependent upon the intensity of the sou'west, be prepared for fishing into a gale—a time you would never want to miss. This means that you should select plugs for their castability rather than for their catchability. Getting hits can be aided by using teasers—usually a small fly or rubber lure in front of the plug.

Only a few hundred yards east of Race Bar are the Traps, where a tide rip forms during the early rise. Often, the very fish that were on Race Bar at low tide have moved to the Traps once rising water began to run. The Traps, however, are not as reliable as the Race.

No examination of this area would be complete without some discourse on Hatches Harbor. This small inlet just south of Race Bar at the lighthouse will sometimes gather stripers in its falling waters, but usually after low tide on the chart, when water is still emptying from the pond. But as it is with the rest of this locale, the situation is dependent upon sand eels moving into the pond. The bowl-shaped curve of the beach between Race Bar and Hatches Harbor can serve as a feeding ground for all sizes of striper.

Once the tide is down four hours, you can cross the harbor on foot and fish as far south as you please into New Beach or Herring Cove (two names for the same place). There are times when there are more bass south of the estuary than above. For this entire area, the formula, in addition to low tide, has always been a hardy sou'west wind. Those without a buggy can get a permit to park overnight for fishing at New Beach and cash in on what I speak of here.

Although sand eels are the prevalent bait here, slim, smallish Finland plugs work best. Or, you can rig a castable Gibbs Swimmer as a casting weight for a teaser rig. Best teasers are either Red Gills or white eel flies tied on a 3/0 hook. Wind permitting, this is an excellent place for fly fishing. And if the wind is a two-flag whole gale, you can heave a bank sinker as a casting weight instead of the plug. It is along this very shore that I learned to heave lead with flies above them when the sea was white.

The tendency to use fresh sand eels as a bait for fishing the bottom is fairly recent here. The center of activity for this has largely been Race Bar, since the park service closed Wood End, where bait fishing had been popular. Consequently, vehicles are often parked two and three deep, with anglers using extra rods and creating such a picket fence of equipment that stripers actually bump lines when they swim past, giving the false signal that a bait has been taken. Along with little room for passing fish, plugging a stretch of beach at Race Bar is often out of the question. But the outer edges—Traps to the east, Herring Cove to the south—remain plug water.

A quarter mile east of the Traps, at Race City, where you'll usually see a number of self-contained (camper) vehicles, there is a tide rip that forms west to east at high tide. "Second Rip" or "Telephone Pole Rip," as it is variously called, is a traditional hot spot for big stripers; they come from the east for the bait and the warm currents that fall from Cape Cod Bay. Best time for this spot is when there is a moon or spring tide pulling, as they produce the greatest exchange of water. Moreover, it helps to have a good sou'west pushing in the same direction to make the water move even harder. I have also found that in midsummer, when nights are short, a 1:00 or 2:00 A.M. high tide leaves enough time for the tide to still be pulling at dawn—that magical period when a dull fire is lighting off in the east and linesides are feedin' and movin' like the Boston girls had the towrope. Always expect a serious run of first bluefish in early August. Perhaps you've already noticed a Provincetown surf itinerary emerging that lets you fish at any stage of the tide. Low tide: the Race; rising: the Traps; late rising: Back Beach; high tide to down three: Second Rip; last of the drop: back to the Race. Check out that rating!

CONTACT TIP: Nelson's Bait and Tackle, (508) 487-0037.

65

Pamet River
Truro, Massachusetts

BEST MONTHS TO FISH: July through October.
RECOMMENDED METHODS: Plugging and fly fishing.
FISH YOU CAN EXPECT TO CATCH: Stripers and bluefish.
HOW TO GET THERE: From Route 6 in Truro, take Castle Road west to the end of Corn Hill Road; walk south along the beach to the river jetties.

Flanked by a pair of jetties, the Pamet River is a large estuary that reaches east into Truro from Cape Cod Bay. The north jetty of the opening is the best side for access. Here there is a parking area, and the walk over sand is only about ¹⁄₁₀ mile. As the largest estuarine inlet for 40 shore miles in either direction, the Pamet can have some good runs of bass at times. This spot has a reputation for producing more schoolies than monsters, but I should always be wary of such generalizations, because sooner or later the big fish do show up, as if only to dispute them.

As for timing and methods, you can find linesides in here at any time in season; but, as at any other spot, they are sometimes not around if there are no baitfish to lure them. Again, it is a case of sand eels or sperling imitations with the smaller plugs and light tackle. Even if it is blowing a gale, this is a great fly-rod spot, because you can sometimes have fish around and behind you. The tail end of the dropping tide is best.

CONTACT TIP: Nelson's Bait and Tackle, (508) 487-0037.

As a north-facing beach, Sandy Neck is wind dependent and has its nights.

66
Sandy Neck Beach
Barnstable, Massachusetts

BEST MONTHS TO FISH: July through October.

RECOMMENDED METHODS: Plugging, sea worms, and fly fishing.

FISH YOU CAN EXPECT TO CATCH: Stripers, bluefish, and some sea-run brown trout.

HOW TO GET THERE: Traveling east on Route 6A, take a left onto Sandy Neck Road about 1½ miles after crossing Scorton Creek. (Over-sand vehicle necessary.)

Sandy Neck is another of the Cape's over-sand-vehicle beaches, this one managed by the town of Barnstable with permit regulations similar to those of other drivable beaches. (See hot spot number 63 for ORV equipment requirements.) ORVs will not be allowed on the beach after 9:00 P.M. and have to be off the beach by 11:00 P.M., except for self-contained campers. ORV or chase vehicle seasonal permits can be bought at the gatehouse during the day for non-residents for $50. No daily fees. Camper or self-contained permits for non-residents are $50 annual with a daily fee of $10.

One of the problems with this area, despite its proximity to both the Canal and Cape Cod Bay, is that as a north-facing beach, it does not often have a surf-favorable onshore wind. Among regular Cape stripermen who have fished the other beaches, Sandy Neck is the least popular. And, while boats in full view of the beach can tong all day long, it is often unaccountably deadsville. The horseflies alone are enough to make a surf fisher renounce this beach for all time.

Scorton Creek, which is at the beginning of the beach, hosts a unique fishery in the form of sea-run brown trout. Best fishing is fall and winter way up the creek during low tide. Use small lures or saltwater fly patterns for well-fed browns, which, though rare, can heft up to 5 pounds.

BREWSTER FLATS

Because of their proximity to Sandy Neck, I feel compelled to mention the Brewster Flats, more as a warning than a numbered hot spot of the Striper Coast. The place is problematic, in that while it can be sensational fishing at times, it is among the most dangerous places you can fish for stripers. I have seen men cry in terror once they got turned around out there in a fog and rising tide. Problem is that this part of Cape Cod Bay is so shallow that it goes dry just long enough to invite an adventurous surfcaster—usually without a compass—onto its vast expanse. Within these flats, you can sometimes find Mr. Linesides trapped in a hole, feeding on sand eels, and you'll catch him when he has no place to run. Then, while putting your fish on a stringer, the water rises an inch and you can no longer tell which water is shallow and which is deep. Worse, what if you drop your flashlight?

The natural limitations of the Brewster Flats, combined with the limited parking opportunities and occasional police hassles, should be enough to make you reassess your priorities. I have lain in my bunk all day waiting for darkness and tide to fish there, and then wondered what it was about this spot that kept me from getting the sleep I needed so badly. Best fishing is midsummer, and tell the Nickerson Funeral Home that Frank Daignault sent you because a surfcaster could easily be killed there.

CONTACT TIP: Just about any Canal tackle shop could advise you on Sandy Neck. Eastman's Sport and Tackle in Falmouth is good. Call (508) 487-0034.

67
Hull Gut
Boston, Massachusetts

BEST MONTHS TO FISH: June through October.
RECOMMENDED METHODS: Plugs and chunk baits.
FISH YOU CAN EXPECT TO CATCH: Stripers, bluefish, and some flounder.
HOW TO GET THERE: At the Route 3A split in Hingham, follow the signs to Hull and Nantasket.

Hull Gut guards the south edge of Boston Harbor/Quincy Bay at the very end of a finger of land that reaches north into the sea.

Consequently, there is a vicious tide rip that forms on both tides. While this rip is sometimes crowded with plug fishers, bait fishers using chunks like to spread along the shore from behind the High School to J Street to X, Y, and Z streets on the late incoming tide and also two hours before low. Serious striper pros like to feed swimmers in the Hull Gut current in the deep night. Be particularly mindful of a shift in stripers at low tide when the water slacks. All fishing faces the east and north, so avoid Hull during a storm. In that event, a great alternate spot is the Fore River under the 3A Bridge, on the Weymouth (east) side. It may be big-city fishing, but the blues like to go there.

In the past this area hosted fantastic numbers of cod, pollack, and flounder, but all that has dropped off to mediocrity, with only a few flounder enduring.

CONTACT TIP: Pemberton Bait and Tackle, (617) 925-0239, knows about Hull Gut.

68
Boston Harbor Islands
Boston, Massachusetts

BEST MONTHS TO FISH FOR STRIPERS: June through October.
RECOMMENDED METHODS: Lures, bottom baits and fly fishing.
FISH YOU CAN EXPECT TO CATCH: Stripers and bluefish.
HOW TO GET THERE: Ferries from several downtown locations.

The Harbor Islands in Boston are a collection of spots where there is camping adjacent to suitable shore fishing. The park service maintains

Boston Harbor Islands are cleaner today and the fishing is better for it.

a ferry service departing from three locations: Long Wharf, Boston; Pemberton Point at Hull; and, Fore River Shipyard, Quincy. Many of the islands are accessed by shuttle boat from Georges Island. You can consult the park ferry schedule by calling (617) 223-8666.

The 1,600-acre Island Park, which boasts 35 miles of shoreline, is jointly managed by the National Park Service, Coast Guard, Massachusetts DEM, MDC, and Mass Water Resources. These Harbor Islands are steeped in tradition and dripping in history; some of them were used as "internment camps," prisons really, and go all the way back to King Phillip's War, the detainment of Civil War Confederate officers and even Italian prisoners of the U.S. during WWII. Back to fishing.

The National Park Service administers a permit system for small tent camping. The camping season here continues through Columbus Day weekend in October on Lovell's, Peddock's, Grape, and Bumpkin. Each of the four islands has ten or more individual sites that have a two-week limit and one or two group sites. To make free reservations, which are required on Lovell's and Peddock's, call (617) 727-7676. Bumpkin and Grape have a reservation fee of around $7 per person and rising for individual sites and $25 for group sites; call (877) 422-6762. You can cook but you have to carry in your own water and carry your trash out. No alcohol or pets are allowed. For more information, call (617) 223-8666 or visit *www.BostonIslands.com.*

Alternative mainland choices would be camping at the campground at Wompatuck State Park in Hingham. Another good south harbor shore fishing option is Hull Gut in Pemberton (which see at spot number 67) where a thin finger of land reaches into the harbor opening that throbs with current and good fishing on either tide.

From the shore of these strategically placed islands, it is possible to fish some hard running tide rips—preferably at night—when striper fishing from shore is at its best and when there are few, if any, others fishing. Tidal exchange is high here, usually over 10 feet, and mid-tide rips worth testing are at the south end of Lovell's. Peddock's Island splits with two south ends. Thus, with the north point, three spots command current on this island. Grape in Weymouth and Bumpkin in Hingham don't appear to offer as much current. Keep in mind that while utilization of the harbor is new, those methods that work elsewhere will stand you well here. Light tackle plug and lure fishing can be as productive as fly fishing. Late-summer bluefish are an added species that always enhances the mix found in striper fishing, and Boston is no exception. On any part of our Striper Coast, fall is the time when fishing really picks up. Late September and early October are prime in this northern part of their range. Our highly migratory stripers are feeding heavily on bait supplies that are higher at this time while more fish are arriving from the north. The remote quality of the harbor islands, when contrasted with the not too far away civilization, is very different and once the ferries end for the night, there is an eerie sense of loneliness.

Downtown Boston is being promoted as a place where people walk—and, when they are not walking, they are taking a water taxi from one part of the harbor to another as well as from island to island. The waterfront is a vibrant, restaurant-filled place mixed with upscale, don't-ask-the-price condos that come with a mooring for your yacht thrown in. Whether you are fishing from a boat or walking an island shore, the more seaward Harbor Islands offer pristine angling opportunities these days for stripers, a species that should surprise no one. There is something counterintuitive about fishing clean water with a big-city skyline behind you and a lineside in your fore. It is a thing that, until I went there, I had never experienced much. It gets you thinking that anything is possible and reminds you how easy it is to lose a good place to fish when the water has no care and that it can be brought back when it has. See the Harbor Islands first before planning an overnight camping trip for fishing.

CONTACT TIP: Consult the park ferry schedule by calling (617) 223-8666.

69

Deer Island, Boston Harbor
Harbor Islands National Recreation Area
Boston, Massachusetts

BEST MONTHS TO FISH FOR STRIPERS: June through October.
RECOMMENDED METHODS: Plugs, other artificials, fly fishing.

FISH YOU CAN EXPECT TO CATCH: Stripers, occasional bluefish.

HOW TO GET THERE: From Revere Beach on the Boston north shore, take the Winthrop Parkway south through Winthrop for three miles to narrowing land at Shirley, then Deer Island will smack you.

Deer Island stopped being an island when the old Shirley Gut was filled by a combination of the 1938 hurricane and fill from the expanding Logan International Airport. Consequently, it is now possible to drive from Winthrop over to the "island," which has become part of the Boston Harbor Islands National Recreation Area with a total of 265 acres with a stunning view from the 2.6-mile harbor walk.

This is no longer your father's Boston Harbor. The Massachusetts Water Resources Authority (MWRA) now treats sewerage from a total of 43 outlying communities that formerly kept the harbor irreparably polluted. No more. Hailed as an engineering wonder, twelve 150-foot giant sludge digesters treat the water before it is piped seven miles out to sea. And the obvious result is a pristine Boston Harbor where water quality is no longer an issue.

Anglers with permits are allowed to fish the beach here after dark. Best currents assemble at the island's end adjacent to the light spire (there is no true lighthouse). A major part of the harbor's tide has to pass here so it is best choice for lure and fly fishers on either the rise or drop. The bottom here might be a little too boulder and weed strewn for bottom baits. While the rip at Deer Island Light is first choice, there can be good plug and fly fishing on the adjacent beaches either side of the light. Back when cod were more of a viable gamefish, Boston Harbor drew a great winter run. If cabin fever or known increases in cod fishing opportunities were to present themselves, I would try bottom fishing here in winter.

CONTACT TIP: Ippi's Bait and Tackle in Lynn, (781) 596-0317.

70

Boston North Shore
Lynn to Gloucester, Massachusetts

BEST MONTHS TO FISH: June through October, but especially July and August.

RECOMMENDED METHODS: Plugs, chunk baits, and fly fishing.

FISH YOU CAN EXPECT TO CATCH: Stripers and bluefish.

HOW TO GET THERE: Leave Route 128 on exit 25 to Route 114 east or, from downtown Boston, travel north on Route 1A. If you have already chosen a destination in this group of hot spots, you'll make better time staying on Route 128. Seeing this area for the first time, use Route 127 north from Beverly for a more coastal drive roughly 10 miles to Gloucester.

This area is an urban collection of nooks and crannies that serious striper locals rely upon to provide steady season-long action. As a place where many go to escape the crowds of Plum Island, the North Shore's secrets are not likely to show up in a book like this one. Starting with Lynn Beach and Red Rock, it is possible to fish dozens of hot spots—some more commonly known than others—in the next 20 or more miles. Devereux Beach in Marblehead is well known for its chunk fishing; Lighthouse Point on Marblehead Neck offers great plug fishing; Winter Island is locally famous for big stripers taken with live bait or chunks; the Danvers River system, which is actually six rivers converging at Salem Harbor, provides inlet fishing at the top of the tide. There is also good bridge fishing, where you can sometimes see big bass in the shadows of the abutments at the Salem Beverly Bridge on Route 107.

Key to working this area is knowing where to park hassle-free or getting to the small public ways first, which is less of a problem at night when you should be fishing. Except for the obvious beaches and marshy inlets, much of what is good here is rocky shore. For those reading water, it is possible to drive the shoreline scenic route around Cape Ann through Gloucester and Rockport. Keep in mind that this east-facing shore is impossible during major storms.

CONTACT TIP: Ippi's Bait and Tackle in Lynn, (781) 596-0317.

There is a reason why Plum Island has such a high rating.

71
Plum Island
Newburyport, Massachusetts

BEST MONTHS TO FISH: May through October.

RECOMMENDED METHODS: Sea worms, plug fishing, chunks, jigs, and
fly fishing.

FISH YOU CAN EXPECT TO CATCH: Stripers, bluefish

HOW TO GET THERE: Coming from the south on Interstate 95, take
exit 57 to travel east on Route 113, then continue until the road
changes to Route 1A into Newburyport, about 3 miles from
Interstate 95. Turning left onto Rolfe's Lane it is about ½ mile
until you take a right onto Plum Island Turnpike (really a back
road) for a mile before going over the Sgt. Donald Wilkinson
Bridge that drops you on Plum Island.

Plum Island is nothing other than a 7-mile sandbar formed by the
eons of flow from the Merrimac River. Most of the surf fishing takes
place at the north end, the river end, which is served by a spacious
parking area. Here you will find regulars gathered at the jetty to the
east and at a sandbar to the north and west: The two spots are just
under a mile apart. Weekends, when the fish are in, you can walk the
shore and see countless lanterns glowing in both directions, marking
the banks of the river.

The rule is that the river mouth (or "Point"), including the jetty
and bar, is best during the dropping tide. During the rise, many
prefer the front beach, which is south of the breakwater. Hands
down, the most popular striper bait is sea worms on the bottom.
Along with traditional worm-fishing methods, Plum Island regulars
of late "work the worms" in river currents, which is a system of
casting egg sinkers above a swivel and leader that leads to a 5/0 to
7/0 baitholder claw hook draped with sea worms. This very effective
bottom-bouncing technique is not likely to be seen elsewhere.

In early spring, about the first week in May, when the first small
stripers usually arrive, jigs have become popular. Later in the month,
plug fishing starts, along with an intensifying interest in fly fishing
the river. Expect bluefish arrivals by early August. By then, chunks—

either menhaden or mackerel—can be used for bait fishing. Striper purists who want their bait to cull blues out stick with worms. All fishing is usually over by October 15, but strays have been taken as late as early November.

A little more than 5 miles of the south end of Plum Island may be traversed by over-sand vehicles. But these days, thanks to the same piping plovers that have closed other fishing beaches, no driving is allowed variably until late summer. Then, nightly permits are issued along with "self-contained" permits for those appropriately equipped. Roughly the same equipment and procedural requirements for beach-buggy use are in place here as elsewhere.

Upriver, this side of Surfland, the Joppa Flats (just west of Woodbridge Island) are extremely popular with fly fishers who wade from the nearby seawall. Low tide is the focus of activity, but when it is good, regulars press the time element by wading out late in the drop and learn from experience when to get out during the rise. Nights on an unfamiliar flat for someone lacking experience here can be scary. The wise surfcaster starts either with a guide or eases into this listening to his or her fears. Know when to get out.

Plum Island is to Massachusetts what Montauk is to New York.

CONTACT TIP: Kay Moulton's Surfland Bait and Tackle, (978) 462-4202, is information central for Plum Island.

NEW HAMPSHIRE

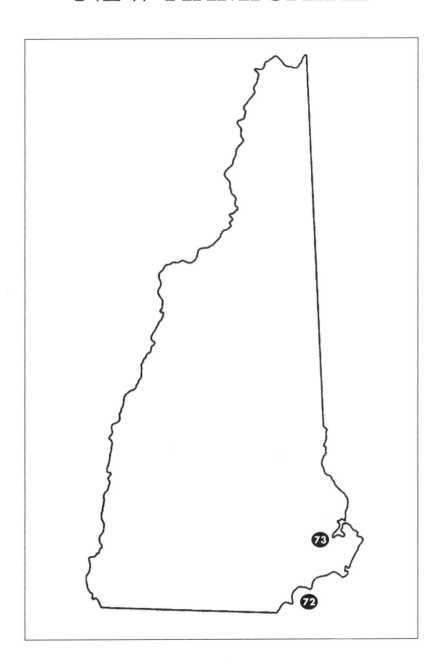

New Hampshire

Gamefish observe no political boundaries and thus are blissfully unaware that the short, 20-mile coastline they forage between Massachusetts and Maine belongs to New Hampshire. This segment of the Striper Coast is small, but it is highly representative of the hydrology of nearby states. For its size, New Hampshire rivals any of the other sections in terms of offering a savory mix of sand, stone, and estuary to lure gamefish.

In this book's preparation, I took into account all the demands of anglers, geography, and natural opportunity; as a result, I could only allow two hot spots from this state, knowing full well that there are more. I have fought the numbers all through the preparation of this work, and New Hampshire sorely tested my shaky ability to walk away from good fishing. Failing to survive the cut, when it could have risen above many others anywhere else on the coast, was Rye Harbor. I'm also certain that the Piscataqua Estuary in Portsmouth—for all its industrial trappings—presents countless shore-fishing opportunities of high order. Lastly, Great Bay hosts a marvelous striper fishery all through the season, which no doubt affords some good shore fishing for those willing to explore. The hydrology of humping tidal exchanges is inspiring, and at these latitudes there are no summer doldrums.

72

Hampton River Inlet
Hampton, New Hampshire

BEST MONTHS TO FISH: Mid-May through early October.
RECOMMENDED METHODS: Plugs, live bait, and fly fishing.
FISH YOU CAN EXPECT TO CATCH: Stripers and bluefish.
HOW TO GET THERE: The Route 1A bridge in Hampton is just over the Massachusetts line on I–95.

This combination of estuary and oceanfront offers six distinct opportunities: sand beach, jetty, and back estuary on both sides of the river. The combination of beach, dunes, oceanfront, and estuary serves the needs of any level of fishing. The jetty offers a chance to reach the tide rips of the river, particularly on a falling tide. However, depending on the wind, these jetties are often wet, and they are always rough going, not to mention slick at low tide. Anglers commonly set up baited rods along the sandy beaches, using bunker or mackerel chunks or freshly dug sand eels. It is possible to walk the grassy shore in the back with a swimming plug after dark and locate feeding stripers by the sounds they make. Don't overlook the protected estuary as a great spot for fly fishing.

All of this is part of Hampton Beach State Park, where ample parking on both sides is never a problem during the night or early-morning hours when you should be fishing. Keep in mind, however, that it is illegal to fish the bridge here. Also, the arrival and departure of bathers during the day in summer—fantastic crowds at both Hampton and Salisbury—unleash rapidly snarling traffic that can trap any unsuspecting fisherman. In late afternoon, or during a sudden shower, the entire world tries to leave all at once.

CONTACT TIP: Hampton Harbor Tackle, (603) 926-1945.

Not for sissies, bridge fishing is highly specialized and Great Bay has a bridge.

73
General Sullivan Bridge
Great Bay
Portsmouth, New Hampshire

BEST MONTHS TO FISH: June through September.

RECOMMENDED METHODS: Sea worms, eels, pogies or bunkers, and bucktail jigs.

FISH YOU CAN EXPECT TO CATCH: Stripers.

HOW TO GET THERE: From either direction on Route 95 in Portsmouth, take the Spaulding Turnpike north toward Newington and Dover. After going over the first bridge, about 3 miles from 95, take Routes 16 and 4 and exit north toward Dover. This turn will lead to parking facilities that are at either end of the General Sullivan Bridge.

Replaced by a larger, more modern span, the roughly 500-foot-long Sullivan Bridge is now a state-managed fishing site—no traffic. Equally important is the fact that this is where the Piscataqua and Little Bay come together. Taking tidal exchange into account, one soon realizes that massive currents mingle in this area to provide ample foraging opportunities. At slack tide, however, stripers—*big* stripers—play a game of musical chairs as they shift positions with changes in the water. Regulars make it a point to be at the bridge when the tide slacks (really less than an hour), to take advantage of moving linesides. Otherwise, full tides of 6 or 8 knots make fishing tough.

I rate this spot high because its potential for a real brute of a striper is matched by few other spots in this territory. Big live baits supported by heavy tackle are in order here. This is no place for a budding amateur to learn the ropes. For instance, it is possible to fish bucktail jigs when the water is speeding up at the eddies in front of bridge pilings to lengthen your time of opportunity. And, depending on the light, you can sometimes see stripers in the bridge shadows, but they face the current and scoot for the bridge's underside after the hook is buried. With a humping tide, no usual strength of line is going to take the combined forces of tide and striper without blood, sweat, and tears at both ends. Better fishermen know how to stretch the time window and when to crank drags down against dangerous pilings, as well as how to deal effectively with heavy lines.

Some 20 years ago, I fished this area from a boat with Dick Pinney, who was kind enough to share this spot with me. At that time, stripers having faded to a mere shadow of their former numbers, we sought coho salmon. Now that the stripers are back, that program has fallen by the wayside, but I learned two things then: that Great Bay is appropriately named, and that Pinney knew both its waters and stripers as well as anyone around.

CONTACT TIP: Sud's and Soda, (603) 431-6320, knows about the Sullivan Bridge.

MAINE

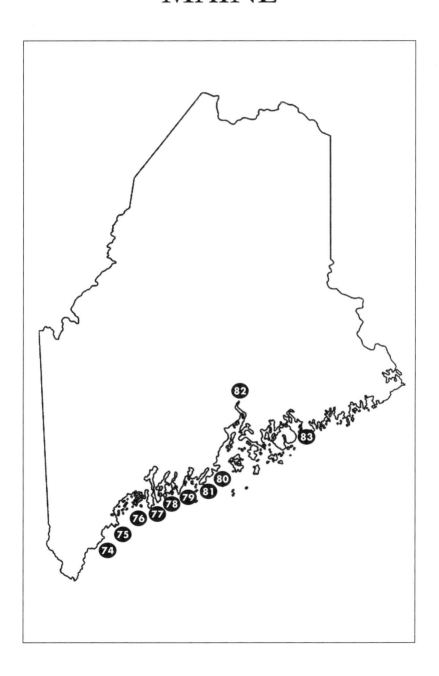

Maine

I have no doubt that one of the weaknesses of this book is its coverage of Maine. In my investigations of that state, I learned quickly that the magnitude of its coastline—when all the nooks and crannies are taken into account—is positively intimidating. It would have served no purpose to try to actually measure the shoreline, but I suspect there are more miles here than in all the other Striper Coast states combined. Therefore, it would not be unreasonable to say that I could easily find one hundred hot spots in its fjords alone. To do so, however, would not be in keeping with my object of providing a usable range of suitable surf-fishing locations in harmony with population needs. As it is, Maine already has more shore fishing that it can use, though the activity is not concentrated on the more southern coasts, as the forthcoming listing might imply. It is rather more evenly distributed, but I lean toward the south end because, since this book must have reasonable limits, I prefer to focus on spots where there are people to utilize them.

Maine's bountiful resources are further enhanced by the view its inhabitants take toward the enjoyment of the outdoors and access to it. In Maine, most landowners would not even look up from their newspapers to concern themselves with a passing sportfisher, unless it was to shout a friendly greeting. Conversely, in most of the states that make up the Striper Coast, shorelines are so jealously guarded that the discreet habits one must use to gain access, such as fishing in the deep of night and hiding one's auto, are as much a part of shore fishing as sharp hooks. Thus, not only does Maine have more, but its people—save for a few newcomers—are more anxious to share it.

Few would find fault with Maine's traditionally intense interest in sportfishing. Indeed, this bastion of outdoorsmanship is known worldwide for its fishing. On closer examination, however, one discovers that Maine's angling traditions do not include saltwater fishing, let alone surfcasting. Indeed, the usual characterization of Maine sportfishing is born of pristine mountain streams and placid lakes teeming with trout and salmon, not a raging surf with linesides darting through the foam. Thus, since both the above pictures are versions of the true Maine, the freshwater bias must be a social rather than natural phenomenon. It might be explained in either of two ways: Perhaps the sportfishers of Maine did not know what they had; or maybe trout and salmon adequately filled their needs. In any case, that is all changing.

Even Maine is beginning to feel the pinch of increased population and the commensurate pressures upon its resources. Traditional anglers find themselves packing and paddling in deeper and deeper each season to escape the crowds. At the same time, they are discovering astonishing fishing opportunities right in their own backyards and in the shadows of some larger cities like Augusta and Bangor. Some of them have to be asking themselves, "Why travel days to the Alligash for a 2-pound brook trout when there are 15-pound blues smoking your fly reel on your lunch hour?" Few will admit it, even to themselves, but the salt-chuck is new fishing for most Mainers. One need only examine the skill levels in evidence to recognize that they've been fishing sweet water a lot longer.

Of course, there are pioneers in saltwater fishing there who are smart enough to smell the coffee of this state's coastal sportfishing potential. Walter Johnson, of Johnson Sporting Goods fame, could never be accused of snoozing in the shadow of mildewing "lobsta pots" after opening four stores, spread from Portland to Rockland— all on the coast and all specializing in saltwater bait and tackle. Another saltwater advocate is Cal Robinson of Saco Bay Tackle Company, who, in addition to spreading the news about shore fishing, has championed offshore fishing for big game species— something Maine seemed to know nothing about until recently.

Besides clean water, let's talk about a few things you won't see anywhere else. The tidal exchange, for anyone coming from below Cape Cod, is huge here at 12 feet in the south and increasing as one travels north. Talk about tide rips! On the other hand, fishing seasons are much shorter than those in, say, Montauk, starting nearly a month later in spring and ending October 15 instead of November 15. With hunting time at hand, it is time to end fishing, even if the fish are still biting. Mainers love their hunting. Lastly, I can't discuss seasons without emphasizing that Maine water temperatures should allay any fears one might have of summer doldrums. Indeed, July and August are the best months to be fishing here.

The cut list for Maine is considerable, but it is a mere fraction of what it could be. Many of the rejected venues easily deserve inclusion as numbered hot spots: Long Beach at York, untold shore stretches on the Kennebec River upstream of Fort Popham, and Reid State Park on Georgetown Island only scratch the surface. Every salmon river in Maine is a suitable striper river. In fact, there are probably more bass caught by salmon fishers—thinking they've just hooked the fish of their dreams—than by those who are really striper fishing. It happens on the Saint Croix River all the time.

Probably the most telling hot-spot story that springs from the boundless legends of Maine culture is the one about the nice couple from "away" (probably Boston) that settled on the woodsy pine shores of Harpswell Sound seeking a kinder life. Not knowing a lot about local fishing, the married couple knew that fishing was around and felt that they had to know more. Out of desperation in their efforts to learn more, they hired a guide to take them out in his boat in the hope of learning more about the striper fishing. They made a few stops at different places until the guide then advised that he was going to hit a favorite hot spot that, while he was reluctant to share it, he felt had the most promise. Whereupon they arrived in the waters just out front of the customer's property to fish.

74

Mousam River
Kennebunkport, Maine

BEST MONTHS TO FISH: June through October.

RECOMMENDED METHODS: Plugs and fly fishing.

FISH YOU CAN EXPECT TO CATCH: Stripers.

HOW TO GET THERE: After using exit 2 of the Maine Turnpike (Route 95), drive Route 9 through Wells to Route 1. Proceed 2 miles north on Route 1, then go right (east) on Route 9 until you see signs on the right for Parsons Beach—about 2 miles.

The Mousam River is a perfect example of the value of estuaries as feeding spots for stripers and blues. This marvelous tidal marsh meanders for many miles inland before the water freshens. Meanwhile, these waters host numerous baitfish while emitting their scent seaward on a dropping tide. That is why regulars here prefer wading the flats on a falling tide in the deep of night, where sometimes moby stripers can be found waiting in the currents of the river. Figure the last three hours of the drop in tide and keep in mind that water will still be dropping from the river long after the ocean front has begun to rise.

According to my experience, when access and size are taken into account, the Mousam is the best of them, but similar local estuaries like the Webhannet River to the south and a few others above could provide yet unmeasured opportunities.

CONTACT TIP: Eldredge Bros. Fly Shop, (207) 363-9269, in Cape Neddick knows about the Mousam River fishing.

Saco River drips with the culture of Maine.

75

Saco River
Biddeford/Saco, Maine

BEST MONTHS TO FISH: June through October.

RECOMMENDED METHODS: Lures and baits.

FISH YOU CAN EXPECT TO CATCH: Stripers and bluefish.

HOW TO GET THERE: From exit 4 of the Maine Turnpike (Route 95), pick up Route 111 east into Biddeford to Route 1.

The Saco River is one of the classic striper and bluefish hot spots in the state. A certain care must be taken in this claim, however, because the reputation was gained largely from boat fishing; otherwise, I would sing its praises even higher. Still, there are any number of hot spots used by surfcasters that can be combined here riverwide.

The Camp Ellis Jetty on the north bank, the Saco side, reaches out into the open Atlantic at the Saco River's mouth. Casts on the south side of this north breakwater would take advantage of falling river currents. In fall, I would check the point where rocks meet the shore on the north side during a north or nor'west wind, as bait and migrating gamefish might tend to gather there.

With plenty of fish in the river, the "Meadow," which is half a mile short of Camp Ellis, is both a protected and productive spot in the river. You'll recognize the Meadow, because it is where the road comes closest to the Ferry Road leading to Camp Ellis. Swimming plugs in the deep night are fine, but if you are a fly rodder, you'll get good results here.

Salmon fishers are sometimes bothered by June stripers at the saltwater barrier of Cataract Dam. You can find this spot from the nearby bridge by looking upstream for the locally famous all-night eatery called Rapid Ray's.

On the south bank, or Biddeford side, some of the locals fish the "Gazebo" behind New England College. Another mile east, at Hills Beach, you'll find the Biddeford Pool, a mile-wide round chamber of salt water; it forms an incredible tide rip during the falling tide. Billy Gardner, my confidant and chief adviser on matters pertaining to Maine, says the Biddeford Pool is a much-overlooked local hot spot. Mush north—"On, you huskies!"

CONTACT TIP: Facts and equipment are available from Saco Bay Tackle Co., (207) 284-4453.

Even the stripers eat lobster when they go to Maine.

76
Old Orchard Beach
Maine

BEST MONTHS TO FISH: July through October.

RECOMMENDED METHODS: Lures, plugs, cut bait, and live eels.

FISH YOU CAN EXPECT TO CATCH: Stripers and bluefish.

HOW TO GET THERE: From any point on Route 1 in Saco, it is possible to follow signs to the Route 9 shore road of Old Orchard Beach.

My old friend John Fleury loves to tell about how the Quebec Frenchmen will show up each season to bathe in the relatively tepid waters of the Gulf of Maine at Old Orchard Beach and invariably end up blitzing bluefish on the sandy beach there. Because this meeting of man and fish is unplanned, it can satisfy any regular's entrepreneurial spirit, as well as his sense of social responsibility, to put surf rods in the anxious hands of the Quebecois—at a rate of ten bucks per fish. Thus, it is possible at times to stroll the sands of Old Orchard, a stack of surf rods on one's shoulder, and end up stowing a bundle of folding green. Many a great bluefish and excited tourist have met under such conditions, the latter crying, "Mon dieu!" as he marveled at his success. There are many seasons in Maine when the bluefish do not migrate that far north. But I am supposed to be telling you more about how you can do this, more likely with stripers.

It is a little over 6 miles from the Camp Ellis breakwater to the Pine Point limit at the mouth of the Scarborough River. At any point along this vast stretch of greater Old Orchard, it is possible to locate stripers and sometimes blues. Naturally, all traditional methods work, but a chunk of mackerel or bunker anchored to the bottom with a fishfinder rig is popular. Also, many Mainers like to fish a live eel along stretches of open beach like this one. During the day in summer, it is not advisable to wrangle with bathers; the nights, however, are quiet, desolate really. Seawater temperatures being what they are here, no conflict is likely in fall. If the tide happens to be dropping, the small inlet at Ocean Park (still Old Orchard) offers an attractive tide rip with waters warmed by the daylight sun that might have the bait to draw gamefish. This estuary is the only break in the straight shore and is a must visit during a night of fishing.

CONTACT TIP: Saco Bay Tackle Co., (207) 284-4453.

77
Scarborough River Marsh
Scarborough, Maine

BEST MONTHS TO FISH FOR STRIPERS: June through September.

RECOMMENDED METHODS: Plugs, live eels and fly fishing.

FISH YOU CAN EXPECT TO CATCH: Stripers.

HOW TO GET THERE: From Route 1 in West Scarborough, take Pine Point Road east for 2½ miles to a bridge over the railroad tracks. Then take a right into the yard of Snow's Canning Factory and follow it around underneath the road beside the tracks for as far as you can until access is blocked for driving. On foot, follow the railroad tracks north for a little over a half mile until you reach a trestle over the river.

This is one of those out-of-the-way spots where only locals go that can produce some truly memorable striper opportunities. The marsh is a wild and unfettered natural setting comprising miles of estuarine grasslands and swamp. Loaded with bait hidey-holes, it is fed by numerous sweet water streams—I stopped counting at 12—that host anadromous baitfish, which are a sure draw for stripers.

Because the marshland almost totally drains with the tide, it is best to fish the late rise and early drop in water, roughly five hours. Again, the locally prevalent bait is best—menhaden or mackerel. Regulars drift dead baits or chunks into the tide from the trestle. In June, when sea worms are hatching out, these could be drifted live-line with clinch on or split shot combinations to achieve the right level in the water column for feeding striped bass. Keep in mind, however, that bluefish, if they arrive at all, don't show much interest in worms. Some striper purists take advantage of this specifically to keep blues away.

CONTACT TIP: The South Portland store of Johnson's Sporting Goods could know about the fishing. Call (207) 773-5909.

78
Spurwink River
Higgins Beach, Maine

BEST MONTHS TO FISH: June through October.
RECOMMENDED METHODS: Plugs, eels, and flies.
FISH YOU CAN EXPECT TO CATCH: Stripers and bluefish.
HOW TO GET THERE: From Route 1, take Route 207 east; at Route 77 (which is also Spurwink Road), turn left and continue to the right turn onto Ocean Avenue at the Higgins Beach sign. Park across the street from the grocery store.

The mouth of the Spurwink is about a ½-mile walk north of the small grocery store on the main road into the seaside village. Parking is available here for a nominal fee during the day and free at night. No public parking is available at the beach.

Where the south edge of the river meets with open water, testy collisions of tide flow and surf occur. Night stripers gather in this sandy section, and surfcasters equipped with waders follow the shallows of a receding tide. The late drop is better, and in order to have this take place during the hours of darkness, high tides of 6:00, 7:00, or 8:00 P.M. are best. You'll often see or hear working fish in the tide rips of your foreground. In the outlet channel, up from the surf, fly fishing can be practiced in comfort, but there are fewer bluefish, as they prefer more open water. To the right of the inlet, clear of the river currents, there are a number of holes that often hold stripers (they change year to year). It is possible to fish bait here, but most of the Spurwink regulars plug, and their favorite time is when the tide is rising again.

CONTACT TIP: The South Portland store of Johnson's Sporting Goods serves the same region. (207) 773-5909.

79
Martin Point Bridge
Presumpscot River
Portland, Maine

BEST MONTHS TO FISH: June through October.

RECOMMENDED METHODS: Live pogies or mackerel (whole or chunks).

FISH YOU CAN EXPECT TO CATCH: Bluefish and stripers.

HOW TO GET THERE: Take exit 9 from Route 295 to Route 1 north. The railroad trestle at Martin Point can be approached via parking areas at either end.

I say blues and stripers in that order, because, when summer action peaks, it's usually with great numbers of bluefish. In spring and fall, it can be stripers, but I saw the spot in early August at a time when every person who had ever hankered for a fish was drifting bait in the rips below the trestle. Crowds were so great that many of the serious locals had devised methods of taking their fish straight up instead of leading them past other anglers to shore. Live pogies or chunks are used, and three hours either side of high tide is favored.

A similar situation exists at the nearby B&M Railroad trestle that guards the opening to Back Cove (get off Route 295 at exit 8). Tidal exchange is not as great, but some locals come here to escape the crowds at Martin Point.

CONTACT TIP: The South Portland store of Johnson's Sporting Goods serves the same region. (207) 773-5909.

The Kennebec River causes the currents of Popham Beach to be productive.

80
Popham Beach
Phippsburg, Maine

BEST MONTHS TO FISH: June through October, but especially July.
RECOMMENDED METHODS: Plugs, chunk baits, and fly fishing.
FISH YOU CAN EXPECT TO CATCH: Stripers, bluefish, and occasional mackerel.

HOW TO GET THERE: Take Route 209 south from Route 1 in Bath and stay on it to land's end at Fort Popham—about 18 miles.

It is a short walk from the ample parking at Fort Popham State Park to the sandy shoreline that is also the mouth of the Kennebec River. Because of the river, there are powerful tide rips here developed by the huge upstream fjord of the Kennebec. As one walks south, or seaward, the currents of the river subside, and the seascape takes on the appearance of a more natural sandy beach. Because of the influence of the river, the area nearly always hosts somewhere between good and amazing numbers of stripers or blues or both. Weekend nights in summer, you can often see the lanterns of anglers stretching south and west with the bend of the beach, waiting for a gamester to come along and take a piece of menhaden or mackerel. They bury sand spikes deep for good reason. Nearer to the fort, where the currents are greatest but the surf lighter, people are inclined to plug. This is also a suitable spot for fly fishing, and, considering the depths (Bath Iron Works launches cruisers into this river), fast-sinking fly lines are advised for best results. The best fishing is the closest, but there are 2 miles of beach for those with a hunter's spirit.

CONTACT TIP: The Brunswick store of Johnson's Sporting Goods, (207) 725-7531, knows the status of Popham Beach. They have three stores, each nearer to their respective hot spots.

81
Morse River
Phippsburg, Maine

BEST MONTHS TO FISH: July through October.
RECOMMENDED METHODS: Plugs and fly fishing.

FISH YOU CAN EXPECT TO CATCH: Stripers and bluefish.

HOW TO GET THERE: From Route 1 in Bath, take Route 209 south, following signs to Popham Beach State Park.

A dune trail from the parking area leads to the sandy shore. Walking right, or southwest, for ½ mile will bring you to the Morse River estuary. This is the gateway to the popular boat-fishing spot for bass and blues called Spirit Pond. Less well known is the fact that surfcasters can walk the flats here at night, whether with plugs or fly fishing, and find excellent numbers of cruising stripers that often betray their presence by slapping bait wildly.

While it is possible to wade nearly all through here safely, the key to doing it right is to operate during the tail end of a dropping tide, but listen to your fears: Get out quickly once the tide starts rising! A no doubt friendly dispute rages among local stripermen as to which is Maine's best, the Morse River or Fort Popham.

CONTACT TIP: The Brunswick store of Johnson's Sporting Goods, (207) 725-7531.

82
Kennebec River
Augusta, Maine

BEST MONTHS TO FISH: June and July.

RECOMMENDED METHODS: Fly fishing, plugs, and jigs.

FISH YOU CAN EXPECT TO CATCH: Stripers and Atlantic salmon.

HOW TO GET THERE: From I–95, take Western Avenue (exit 30) for 1½ miles east to State Street (Route 27). About a mile north on State

Street, take a right onto Bond Street and drive down to the river. There is public parking behind the Eagles hall.

Below the dam in Augusta, stripers of up to 20 pounds show early each June and stay until early July. Fishing here is really freshwater, if tasting it is the criterion. By law, however, the river is considered tidewater below the dam, so no freshwater fishing license is required. This fishery is composed of mostly undersized school stripers, the source of which remains unknown. Because the Kennebec has its own nonmigratory population of stripers and is known to be visited by migratory bass as well, the fish you'll experience here are no doubt a combination of both groups.

The great numbers of stripers here were discovered in the late seventies by salmon fishers who gather on the riverbanks each June, particularly at the mouth of Bond Brook. While the Kennebec is not managed as a salmon river, insofar as there are great numbers of juvenile stock-outs, hundreds of Atlantics show up each spring. Fishery managers theorize that these salmon probably were released in the nearby Penobscot and have mistakenly returned to the wrong river—an anomaly of salmon behavior that is not all that uncommon and that encourages the natural distribution of their population. Similarly, brown trout are often caught here on an incidental basis. I point this out to explain why stripermen sometimes catch salmon, and why salmon fishermen often—much to their dismay—catch stripers. Incidentally, if you are serious about salmon fishing, your methods must be limited to fly fishing, and you must have a salmon license even in tidewater. Also, stay up to date on salmon regs as they are always being refined.

CONTACT TIP: I've had good luck with both Kennebec Guns, (207) 622-1157, and Play It Again Sports, (207) 621-9968.

The Penobscot River salmon fishery also yields stripers.

83
Penobscot River
Bucksport to Bangor, Maine

BEST MONTHS TO FISH: June and September.

RECOMMENDED METHODS: Fly fishing and plugs.

FISH YOU CAN EXPECT TO CATCH: Stripers and Atlantic salmon.

HOW TO GET THERE: Take Route 1A south from Bangor to Prospect Street, then east on Route 174 to the Bucksport Bridge, which leads to Verona Island. Just before the next bridge, take a left to a public boat-launching ramp where locals fish in view of Bucksport, which is across the river.

This tidewater section of the Penobscot River is split by Verona Island. The narrowest side, called East Channel, which is an easy-to-use rocky shore, presents the best tide rips, particularly during a falling tide. The spot is popular enough to attract a steady level of visitation. Folklore puts the best fish seen here around the low forties. The Bucksport/Verona Island shoreline is fjord-like conifer forest and largely undeveloped. Stripers can be found on any part of Penobscot Bay, but this is one of the more reliable and accessible locations.

I first learned of the striper opportunities here while salmon fishing 25 miles upstream in Bangor at the Bangor Salmon Pool. It is a popular spot for schoolie fishing by the mid-June arrival time. This brackish area has a distinct tide and entertains linesides all day and night. Upstream a mile, beneath the Veazie Dam and clear of ocean influence, salmon fishers catch small striped bass incidental to their business. Again, as with the Kennebec (hot spot number 82), no license is needed for linesides, but a salmon license and fly fishing are requirements for salmon.

At Veazie, the best fishing is for Atlantic salmon, which begins May 1 but doesn't really get going until the first June runs of sea-run salmon. In its nineteen eighties glory days, the Penobscot provided an annual return of 3,000 to 6,000 mature fish, which were the results of a half million or more juvenile stock out. Now a mere handful of hangers-on fish for what little natural reproduction took place that survived the high seas nets—only a few hundred 4- to 16-pounders per season. Current regulations do not permit keeping salmon and regulations may vary. Total protection of salmon is also in the wind.

CONTACT TIP: Van Raymond Outfitters, (207) 989-6001, in Brewer is likely to know more about the Penobscot.

USING YOUR HEAD TO GAIN ACCESS

One of the reasons why surfcasting does not enjoy the popularity of boat fishing is that access to the shore can be an interminable nightmare. Before long, the serious surfcaster realizes the truth: he is not wanted at the shore. No kidding.

After gaining permission to park, you can walk a public beach to be attacked by a 90-pound Lab that rips the waders off you. After a successful night of fishing, exhausted from lack of sleep and the night-long bullying of a relentless surf, you drag yourself—and a fish—back to your car to find that it has been towed. And you, certain that it presented no problem to anyone at that hour, know that the tow-truck operator isn't going to give it back until you hand over a day's pay in towing and storage charges that will be split between him and the police officer who called him.

Here in the Northeast, there are places where deeds, first drawn and granted by a king, extend out to sea a specified yardage past the low-water mark, where it would take a diver to drive a stake and where even a passing boat could be cited for trespassing. I know of a spot in Westport, Massachusetts, where somebody was shot and killed for refusing to leave such a place. And, while I could cite numerous examples, I think I have made enough of the lengths to which coastal dwellers will go to retain control not only over that which they own, but over all that they can see. The truth is that coastal habitation is fraught with distrust for outsiders, and, once you have had some exposure, a pattern of conspiracy emerges in which entire societies seek to exclude all others with the help of their police.

Indeed, anyplace where the law fails to accomplish this purpose, other means are quickly devised to serve the ultimate goal of "exclusivity." So-called public rights-of-way are grown over with rustic-looking ivy or blocked with stones; often signs that might have indicated an access to the shore are mysteriously "missing." Frequently, local governments work closely with landowners to make certain that anyone with a place to park has no place to walk, and vice versa.

There is also something inherently evil about the night—the very time when surfcasting is best practiced. Unaccountably, as a culture we remain marvelously close to our witch-burning forebears. Anyone who is enthusiastic about nighttime pursuits is deemed evil, immoral, or at least up to no good. Thus, anyone fishing at night is stigmatized by a clear presumption of guilt. Let's face it: We have a seemingly insurmountable set of social and legal obstacles before us if we want to fish the beach.

How, then, are we to cope with this access situation if we mean to go on surfcasting? Use access regulation to our advantage.

First, fish the deep of night in the more sensitive areas. Avoid movement during change of police shifts—usually midnight. Of course, hide your vehicle and be prepared to walk farther than normal in order to separate the two elements of parking and fishing, which the authorities have so inevitably linked in their minds. So often when fishing I have had police ask me where I was parked. I tell them I was dropped off.

In most cases, though not all, police officers are uneasy about hassling fishermen. They know—better than anyone—that the world is too full of miscreants and malefactors lurking in the shadows for them to be bothering some poor person who has worked all week and now wants no more than to enjoy a few hours of harmless fishing. As a result, it is often possible to appeal to a police officer's better side once he or she understands that you are fishing. This, of course, is dependent upon your behavior, your manner during any exchange, the officer's predisposition, and the extent of your transgression.

Drink always erects barriers. If you have a vehicle full of empties and a little of the stuff on your breath, you are going to be kicked out and then asked to take a Breathalyzer test 100 yards down the road.

Everyone is intimidated by a crowd, not just police. When you fish with five other people, enforcement tends to assert itself more. Conversely, a person who is alone is less of a threat, less likely to inspire resistance or confrontation.

All public beaches forbid sleeping in a vehicle. This is important information for surfcasters, who practice their craft at all hours. We all have experienced slow fishing on a night when the sandman was nudging. By tradition, a fellow sitting up wearing waders—even if his eyes are shut—is resting; but if his body falls during the onset of rapid eye movement, he is sleeping. Going horizontal can get you kicked out. Of course, surfcasters have an easier time keeping a low profile because of night fishing. Locals, whether they own the land or not, can't harass you if they themselves are sound asleep. Don't wake them with a beer party.

The level of sophistication in policing today dwarfs what was in evidence only a generation ago. I have vivid recollection of police threatening to lock people up for "being a smart aleck." Barrington, Rhode Island, used to enforce an ordinance against all street parking in the town. I recall late-night "routine checks" (since struck down by the Supreme Court) in which we—there were three of us, one an off-duty police officer—had to explain where we were going and what we were doing—with six surf rods on the roof! On Nauset Beach, as recently as twenty years ago, a police officer would spend the night warning all drivers with New York tags that he would cite them for speeding if they didn't slow down; he never did this to anyone from Massachusetts. While this might explain my attitudes, at least in part, I hasten to add that such outrages today are less likely. What you'll get now is a more thought-out, better-planned heave-ho.

Sometimes, it is possible to raise the stakes if (1) you are prepared to engage an attorney, or (2) you *are* an attorney. I was once ordered to remove my vehicle from an, ahem, "private road" by a police officer when I knew the town plowed it every time it snowed. I held my wrists out and told him to arrest me. He didn't, but what if he had? I have repeatedly been confronted with situations where I could have gone to court with representation and made fools of the local authorities. But is that the price you want to pay for a night of fishing? To a great extent, it's a bluffing game, and police dread having to go to court to defend their actions when they are as arbitrary and capricious as they sometimes seem. Of course, when the towns are bluffing it doesn't go that far, but it still spoils your night. And they only go on to do it to somebody else.

But don't overlook the fact that you may lack the legal judgment to pick the right situation for taking on the law. You could simply be wrong.

The impression that a discussion like this one tends to generate is that the beach is perpetually guarded by armed uniformed security forces dragged along the seascape by hungry, panting, razor-toothed guard dogs, but that is only true west of Montauk and at a progressively diminishing level east of there. Fact is, the farther up the Striper Coast one goes, the less validity there is to the notion that access is even a problem worth talking about. My old surfcasting friend Ken Hancock, a Connecticut native with a measure of striper blood in his veins, says, "It is impossible to be on the beach at night in this state unless you know someone with waterfront property." On the other hand, the Rhode Island shore presents a changing picture where hope for access begins to surface. This hope later flourishes (with certain notable federal exceptions on Cape Cod) to the point where you can fish the night naked without embarrassment by the time you get to the rockbound coast of Maine. Not only is there hope, there is surfcasting at any hour, with any number of rods, with any friend you might choose.

TEN COMMON SURFCASTING ERRORS

1. Failure to fish at night, particularly for stripers.
2. Use of tackle that is too light.
3. Lack of suitable contingencies for landing a world-class striper. Being unprepared.
4. Poor knots.
5. Hooks that are too large.
6. Dull hooks.
7. Failure to understand natural, environmental conditions and their interrelationships with fishing.
8. Listening to people speculate about where the fish are or what is happening when they don't have a clue.
9. Use of rancid or unfresh baits.
10. Failure to read the water.

PLACES IN TIME

The familiar feeling of thinking that I've said it all visits me at the close of each book. With seven striper titles in print and still counting, when you have walked the bays and beaches all your life with a surf rod, there is so much to say. Thinking about that, time itself is a subject deserving of treatment.

We can all be thankful that this enigmatic last item remains as wild as the wind and the sands pushed about by it, because the magical relationship between time and place will never be uncovered nor understood. It would be a bad thing for fishing if it were. We all are victims of time, all served by it. We all are wise enough to save it. We are all experienced enough to recognize that each place we visit, for whatever purpose, is never the same on a different day. Time is the one thing that we will never fully understand, regardless of how well we fish or how well we choose our places. Time is too subjective, too fleeting, too different with each day that passes. But most of all, time was the thing I was once not smart enough to fear.

Time was when I worried about two things: I worried that we would lose our fish, and I lamented that soon we might have no place where we could try for them. Now, some forty years later, we have as many fish as we've ever had in my lifetime, and there are still plenty of beaches. But tell me, where did the time go?

It seems as if it were only yesterday when I first found the special magic at The Stone, a place that for me has been symbolic of the passage of time and which I have known since my youth as a surfcaster. I am comfortable with the spot because I have been there many times when the tide was pulling to the east and felt the line straighten from the current. Just often enough, there has been a big striper there that has taken my offer and moved off.

The Stone is one of those special places that is reliable enough to make you want to go back; or, if you've been fishing the area, it is a place no competent surfcaster would want to pass up. Fact is, if the spot has any failing, it is that a few very good surfcasters know about it. Even nights when I had thoroughly scratched it, it always made me uneasy to see somebody come in late and test it for even a few casts. One never knew when a migrating striper might take it over. My selfish, overly possessive feelings about it bordered on the unhealthy—the idea of somebody else fishing my Stone!

Of course, it was not a spot that would hold only one fish. Once, on a big-water night during a new moon, a sou'west humping against the beach, big stripers were stacked in a current there, and I caught them until I ran out of eels. Only once. And that was so long ago; things were different then. That was before limits and concern for striper conservation.

I share a lot of memories with The Stone, but something—thanks to time—is changing our relationship. Many nights, on mid-watch hunts for striped bass, I resent each prod that the spot influences upon my memory. There is now something sad about The Stone, but not because it has changed. Enriched with the sensitivities of age, I am reminded by it all too well of a greater autumn than the one I am fishing.

I go to the spot much in the way another person might attend Mass. It is an almost unconscious acknowledgment of the seasons for me. In its inscrutable hold upon me, it is something of an altar of surfcasting that I am unaccountably compelled to respect, if for no other reason than an unrelenting past. There remains a here and now to each encounter with The Stone, but I am always visited by the memories that seem to inspire both an abiding sentimentality and extra effort. As always, the ritual remains a well-cast line with the express purpose of a fine striped bass.

Tonight, the ritual starts with a barely discernible change in wind, spitting snow in harmony with a drop in barometer and temperature. I know that I am shrugging off the season, immersed in some pretense, some inner conflict, that I'm really not supposed to care. And while there is cold in the night, the heat of summer lingers. I can feel the difference in my waders, see it from the sea smoke that hovers inches above the surface while the snow dances and darts into the gray fore.

The Stone is a good distance this year. Not that it ever moves, but the beach builds sand one year, takes it away another. There have been times when I could not reach it with an eel. Others, when it was too close, too accessible. This year, if I pressed my waders in a gentle surf, I picked up enough yardage to lay a bait far enough past it to be certain that I was covering it right. That is what I had done.

I wasn't bringing the eel in, just taking some of the line that the surf had left, when I felt a suspicious drum. Stepping forward so as to throw slack, I pushed the clutch, unconsciously positioning my right thumb to stop any override. The line lifted, then spun from the reel in long thrusts, as the take moved off in a series of erratic dashes. Then I engaged the gears, waited for the line to lift, and came back with the stick while stepping a yard backward with a shift in weight. There was some panic at the other end, a testing of what strange antagonism had beset it, then line moved against the drag.

Backing from the surf, I could feel the powerful surges of the lineside as its body straightened and flexed toward the outside against the line, as though something were whacking it. Dry braid left the spool now, but I felt no apprehension. Soon it would slow, trying a change in direction, and I would put it back on the reel. But now was the violent part, the time when the fish would test my equipment. It was important now to give it its way for a few minutes so it would tire and I could then take over. We had done this so many times that I was beginning to feel I was a character in a play, and that not even the fish had changed. The yards came easily; some left the spool grudgingly, the line's ownership shifting between us. The bass moved west along the beach a short distance while I followed, cranking. Then I made out the dorsal just outside, rising with each bulge in the sea. I pressured, the fin disappeared in a brief, spent struggle, and I hauled back gently just as the foam built and washed to shore. The oval form slid almost motionless in the white suds, and I kept it high long enough to ground it on the wet sand—then a few fast steps and a grasp of the lower jaw.

Years past, I might have unsheathed the rusty pick from my belt and pressed it into the lineside's skull, its pectorals extending briefly. Then I would have lifted the fish, carried it to where I had left my kit at the dune base, and buried it to keep anyone from seeing it. No more. Such rituals are as anachronistic as the gray-haired old man being watched from my boots. Lucky striper, it has resumed its freedom and migration.

This was a delicious time for me as I sat beside my things, my back against an eroding dune that slipped loose sand crackling against my parka. There was no need for another fish, I thought, while unwrapping a sandwich. The hot coffee burned a little, as if trying to fight an impending chill that might threaten this memorable time at the empty shore. Nothing on the outside, nothing in the sky. Even buggy tracks had been smoothed by the westerlies that were straining to change the seasons. I couldn't shake the feeling that there were two of us: a graying old man who struggled with the sea and another who could watch him as if exempt from all ravages while indulging in the joys of contemplation.

There might be another fish at The Stone, I thought, but if I quit now, I could leave with the feeling that I had triumphed over it again. I dared not risk languishing a winter in defeat. Walking down sans rod in one last ritualistic gesture, I watched a wave kiss the tip of The Stone. Trying to remember all that I could store, I savored the scent of rotting weed and salt, felt the last relative warmth of the water, heard the last rhythmic hiss of a season's surf while resisting the fearful urge to count remaining departures.

The silence of the snow, the loneliness of the shore, that last-man-on-earth feeling that I have known so many times before, never to be experienced again in quite the same way—it's something that you can never re-create in your mind. I know, because I have tried at night in bed when I foolishly sought to program my dreams. It is a drug that comes of its own calling, like the snow, where man has no control. I have thought of this many times, and I am certain that the only power we have is to go to the places where it is most likely to happen. I knew then, when I turned my face to the east and pulled my hood back to let the snow anoint me this one time more, that I was experiencing a feeling and a place so fleeting that I could never hope to have it quite the same way again.

Whipping my four-wheeler along the waterline trail toward dinner, my warm wife, and home, I thought of Devlin's Tap for a brandy and beer. Drafts are always so good in those old-time, little neighborhood taverns that date themselves with ladies' entrances. By now the snow was swirling so hard that it mingled white on white with the breaking surf. I thought of trying for another big fish, knowing that I could have made a thousand casts, landing who knows how many bass and blues, but the weather had me edgy, and I had had enough.

Once at Devlin's, I was beginning to think, it would be a certainty that some mackinaw-clad local cracker, partway in his cups, noticing my waders and the snow, would stage-whisper that it takes all kinds. And I planned, because Lord knows I've done it many times before, to raise my glass in a subtle toast and wink at him for what he had missed.

PICK OF THE MONTH

Here is a calendar of hot spots:

February: Providence River (number 30)
March: Thames River (number 14)
April: Sound View Beach (number 11)
May: Enfield Dam (number 7)
June: Charlestown Breachway (number 21)
July: Race Point (number 64)
August: Popham Beach (number 80)
September: Plum Island (number 71)
October: Nauset Beach (number 58)
November: Narragansett (number 26)

BEST IN SPECIES

Here is a list of locations that are best for each of the following commonly sought species:

Striped bass: Cape Cod Canal (numbers 52 to 55)
Bluefish: Wasque Point (number 43)
Blackfish: Bristol Narrows (number 34)
Fluke (summer flounder): Beavertail (number 28)
Porgy (scup): East Beach (number 20)
Bonito: Inlet to Great Salt Pond (number 41)
False albacore: Vineyard Bridges (number 42)

USUAL AND CUSTOMARY REQUIREMENTS FOR AN OVER-SAND VEHICLE

The following items and accepted modes of behavior are usual for acquisition of permits to drive over sand. These requirements—sizes, strengths, and ratings—vary from one jurisdiction to another and are intended only to be representative of what is needed for a beach permit.

- Shovel (heavy duty military or entrenching)
- Tow rope or chain
- Jack and support stand
- Street-legal tires (snow or mud tread often rejected)
- Spare tire
- Low-pressure tire gauge (0–20 lbs.)
- First-aid kit (Coast Guard approved)
- Fire extinguisher (CG or ICC approved)
- Road flares
- Flashlight
- Auto insurance
- Four-wheel drive

All driving must be on prescribed dune trails or on the front beach.

Avoid bathing areas and other examples of user conflict.

Stay out of the dunes or any areas where vegetation might be compromised.

All beaches have speed limits, which vary from 5 to 15 m.p.h.

Ruts or holes caused by stuck vehicles must be filled and any debris removed.

No outside passengers (usually in the form of tailgate sitters).

Headlights must be used at all times.

Avoid bird nesting areas and stay out of marked areas.